Fostering Writing in Today's Classroom

Authors

Richard Gentry, Ph.D.

Jan McNeel, M.A.Ed.

Vickie Wallace-Nesler, M.A.Ed.

Foreword by

Laura Robb, Hon. Ph.D., M.S.Ed.

SHELL EDUCATION

Image Credits

Vickie Wallace-Nesler
Bob Brown of Brown's Photography

Shell Education

5301 Oceanus Drive
Huntington Beach, CA 92649-1030
http://www.shelleducation.com

ISBN 978-1-4258-1190-7
© 2014 Shell Educational Publishing, Inc.

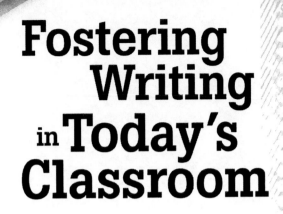

Fostering Writing in Today's Classroom

Table of Contents

Foreword

Fostering Writing in Today's Classroom is a professional book you'll want to keep close at hand because it contains everything you need to set up and facilitate a productive writer's workshop! You'll find yourself continually referring to specific lessons, reviewing the excellent forms that support students as they complete notebook entries, gathering and organizing ideas for student writing, or setting goals for revising content and editing for conventions. Teachers will appreciate the suggestions for setting up a writer's workshop classroom, the excellent management tips in each chapter, the sample activities and detailed charts, as well as the literacy snippets from classrooms. The questions under "Reflect and Review" at the end of each chapter are also very beneficial because they encourage self-reflection and conversations with colleagues.

Advantageous to novice and experienced teachers is the detailed chapter, "Developing the Traits of Good Writing." The authors demonstrate the importance of speaking a common language when discussing the quality characteristics that define excellent writing. For each of the traits of good writing—ideas, organization, voice, sentence fluency, word choice, and presentation—the authors provide detailed suggestions and approaches for teaching, questions to use with students when conferring with them about the trait, and scaffolding suggestions. They also include charts that support teaching the traits and forms that deepen students' understanding of each trait. The chapter ends with a chart, "The Writing Process and Writing Trait Connection," that shows how the traits link to the five stages of the writing process. Not only will this chart support teachers, but it will also encourage students to consider specific traits as they move through the writing process.

Teachers will also treasure this book because it includes a chapter on using inquiry-based learning and close reading to support writing across the curriculum. They will appreciate the charts on formats that work for different disciplines and discussions of casual, semi-formal, and formal writing that work across the curriculum. Content teachers will find the chart on "Creating Formal Writing Assignments in the Content Areas" filled with a myriad of choices that can make writing meaningful and engaging for students. Additionally included is a chart about the five phases of beginning writing, spelling, and reading and indicators that enable you to identify each phase, as well as tips for matching students to a phase.

The heart and soul of this book is about writer's workshop. The authors become your personal guides as you navigate each stage of the writing process. Because of their rich and varied teaching and coaching experiences, the authors anticipate and address questions about workshop at various stages of the process. I love the additional recommendations for professional reading for each chapter because these celebrate the need for ongoing learning of best practices.

This must-have book will become your source for everything related to writing workshop. Like me, you'll find yourself repeatedly rereading sections. Equally important, you'll gain the tools necessary to support your student writers by using praise and encouragement and building on what each child does well.

—Laura Robb, Hon. Ph.D., M.S.Ed.
Author of *Unlocking Complex Texts* and
Teaching Reading in Middle School

Dedication

In memory of Donald Graves (1930–2010)

He inspired generations of writing teachers.

He lifted up children as writers.

His voice echoes from our pages.

Introduction

Take Your Craft to a Higher Purpose and a Greater Accomplishment

 Teach writing. Empower the child. Change the world.

Teaching writing is of vital importance for every teacher in today's classrooms. At no time in recent history has fostering writing in the classroom been more crucial. Propelled by powerful research, including brain scan studies linking writing to reading and thinking, student writing is recognized as being critical for learning and crucial for every child's academic and future career success. In 21st century classrooms, every teacher must be a writing teacher.

This book is intended to be your guide—an inspirational, research- and evidence-based, practical, and accessible compendium to living the life of a writing teacher and fostering the love, need, and life-changing effects of everyday writing in your classroom. For pre-service and novice writing teachers, the foundations you need to get started and move forward are provided. Master teachers will find fresh ideas and enlightenment sprinkled with quotes from the eminent leaders of our craft. This book will help you take the craft of writing to a higher ground.

As we travel across the United States and beyond, we work in many districts where legions of teachers—not well-prepared to teach writing, through no fault of their own—have been thrust into turmoil with high expectations and demands for teaching writing but are given no staff development, no resources, and little support. This book is their guide.

Fostering Writing in Today's Classroom takes a process approach as you become a master writing teacher and your classroom becomes an apprenticeship for training a new generation of writers. Even if you don't feel confident as a writing teacher today, we will show you the way. Writing is often frightening to students. It requires stamina and resilience. Yet it's the job of every student to write. Your apprenticeship will enable your students to get the job done.

If you follow this guide, your classroom will not be a stage with you lecturing up front. Instead, your writing classroom will be a haven for students to develop their voice, trust you to help them express what they feel, explore their passion, and think and speak with confidence. You will be that kind of writing teacher—the kind who is not just the judge but the type of writing teacher who inspires by advocating for students.

Fostering Writing in Today's Classroom follows a research-based workshop model for writing instruction and goes beyond the workshop to incorporate writing across the curriculum. It provides opportunities for students to make choices and develop as independent writers and thinkers. This workshop model dedicates more time to showing students how to write and less time telling students what to do, grading papers, or implementing writing-test prep. Students will be shown how to write to learn and time will be spent on mini-lessons and conferences demonstrating, modeling, and meeting the individual needs of students, which is not only good for your students but invigorating for you. In the wise words of master writing teacher Nancie Atwell, "The workshop is the best, maybe the only, truly differentiated approach to teaching and learning. Here, students can act and are known as individuals. Here, teachers recognize and support the needs and growth of individual students" (2008, 6). *Fostering Writing in Today's Classroom* shows you how to accomplish this goal. We'll show you how to coach, inspire, and guide your students to become the best writers they can be.

Chapter 1 starts with the first question teachers ask when we meet them: "How do I set up my classroom for writing?" We show you how to organize space for group meetings, arrange tables or desks for writing and peer conferencing, organize materials, display publications, and plan space for conferences and small groupings.

Chapter 2 explains how to manage your writing classroom by including sample schedules, routines, and frequently asked questions. Students learn by doing, and management is at the very core of any successful classroom.

Chapter 3 digs deeply into teaching writing as a process. We scrutinize the five-step writing process and go beyond to review the history of the writing process as a revolutionary movement, gleaning wisdom from its founder, the late Dr. Donald Graves.

Chapter 4 explores the natural beginnings of writing, reading, and spelling. We focus on the early reading and writing connection, spotlighting the beginning developmental phases of reading and writing in primary grades. No teaching writing compendium would be complete without full consideration of elevating writing skills using close reading, inquiry-based learning, and writing across the curriculum. **Chapter 5** focuses on spiraling upward with writing to learn and writing in the disciplines, including episodes and lesson suggestions for writing across the curriculum through grade eight.

Best practices are the foundation of this work. Both the writing process and the traits of quality writing are fully covered in *Fostering Writing in Today's Classroom*. **Chapter 6** demonstrates how and why to teach ideas, organization, word choice, sentence building, voice, and conventions with sample lessons. **Chapter 7** rounds it all off with new directions in writing instruction, including the impact of technology, the resurgence of cursive handwriting, and best tips for struggling writers.

Fostering Writing in Today's Classroom is layered with the research base you need to have confidence, but it is our goal to give you the best practices, tips, how-to guides, answers to your questions and concerns, and a report on trends for the future all wrapped into one easy-to-read book. We hope to support teachers through 30 years of synthesis of research, served on a plate of practical advice from our work with master teachers and our combined 100 years of working with thousands of students in the classroom.

Read this book. Tell your colleagues about it. Teach writing. Change the world.

Chapter 1

Setting Up Writer's Workshop

 "The classroom environment you create has a profound effect on the social, emotional, physical and intellectual development of the children you teach."

—Susan Schwartz (1991, 9)

While visiting classrooms, we often ask students to share what they do during their writer's workshop. Many responses from younger writers include "make pictures, read and write, write all kinds of stories and make them into books, and share our stories with each other." Older students respond, "We write, plan our ideas, practice in our notebooks, share our writing, write, revise and edit, look at how an author did something in their book, and score our writing." In these classrooms, it is a rare occasion to hear "the teacher teaches" because the actual teaching is often seamless and transparent in the context of the student's craftsmanship as a writer. In writer's workshop, students are valued and respected as writers and are provided an environment with rituals and routines that nurture and support the act of writing. These teachers create a community of writers where writing is the focus in a classroom that includes space for whole-group instruction, space for working in groups, a place for both individual and peer conferences, convenient materials storage, and access to other resources that students need for writing. Harvey Daniels (2004) tells us, "The workshop model is simple and powerful. It derives from the insight that children learn by doing…" (152). He advocates that teachers who "organize subject matter, time, space, materials, students, and themselves to make learning happen" (10) facilitate successful classrooms. Creating a well-organized classroom along with mini-lessons that teach students expectations and routines will go a long way in developing the environment necessary for nurturing independent and successful writers.

Teachers often request support in setting up their classrooms for writer's workshop. Ms. Parks, a traditional fifth-grade teacher, asked for guidance as she moved into a workshop-teaching model. The first suggestion was to sketch a layout of the physical room, identifying any stationary objects, windows and closets, and doors as shown in Figure 1.1.

Figure 1.1 Layout of Physical Classroom

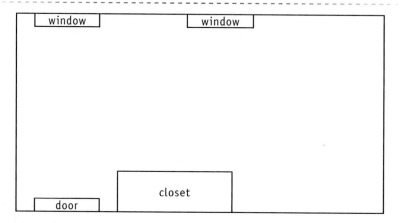

Figure 1.2 models the second step in designing the layout of the classroom. Here, sticky notes label the classroom layout with the essential components of writer's workshop: whole-group instruction, small-group conferences, peer conferences, spaces for sharing, the writing/publishing center, and materials. Management mini-lessons explicitly clarify the purpose of procedures for each space. Some areas, like peer conferences and publishing, are added later as teachers and students become comfortable with writer's workshop. A large area for a group meeting is essential for whole-group instruction. If possible, a document camera, an interactive whiteboard, or a projector are used for demonstrations.

Figure 1.2 Layout of Physical Classroom with Sticky Notes

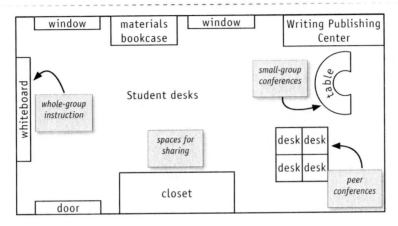

Tubs, baskets, and containers are gathered to organize materials and resources by genre or content area. Writing supplies are pulled from the supply cabinet and neatly stacked in labeled containers for easy student access. Using Ms. Parks's class roster, we look at student assessment data from the previous year and develop a grouping chart arranged to accommodate the strengths and weaknesses of each student. With this information, the furniture is arranged into small clusters of three to five student desks to promote collaboration and provide for easy movement between areas. The small-group conferences table is placed so that Ms. Parks can scan her group during conferences for both positive and negative behaviors and maintain eye contact at all times. In addition, suitable areas that will support a variety of sharing activities are identified. In visualizing the classroom in action with Ms. Parks, the overall physical setup is considered and the room is checked for workspace, physical comfort, and accessibility of writing materials and resources. Over the next few days, the effectiveness of the arrangement is noted, and any modifications needed are made to create areas where students become self-motivated, engaged, and independent problem-solvers.

In the sections that follow, we provide suggestions for setting up your writer's workshop. It is through our personal training and experiences, along with visits and conversations with both novice and seasoned teachers, that we make these recommendations. Developing a space that is comfortable during modeling and writing and provides safe movement while gathering materials, conferencing, and sharing requires careful planning. As you read on, consider your teaching and management style as you adopt the writer's workshop model, adapt it to the developmental level of your students, and make it your own.

Spaces

"The writing workshop is a highly structured place. There have to be all kinds of management structures in place for students to know how it works and how the workshop will be maintained."
—Katy Wood Ray with Lester L. Laminack (2001, 14)

Whole-Group Meeting Area

With our background as consultants working in many classrooms and making observations of room design, we encourage teachers to gather students into a large meeting area for a daily writing mini-lesson. The meeting space should be comfortable, inviting, large enough to accommodate all students, and flooded with writing anchor charts. Not only does the movement to and from the gathering place give students a body and brain break, but once they have gathered near, you will notice fewer distractions, less negative behaviors, and increased engagement. Students need close proximity to a partner to look, lean, listen, and talk, yet they can be allowed their own personal space. When space is limited, closely gather half of the students and allow others to sit in chairs located directly behind them. The mini-lesson area should be designed so that all students have a view and can observe an explicitly modeled session. Then, engage in a conversation. When modeling a mini-lesson, sharing resources, or discussing student writing samples, it is important to have materials well organized and easily accessible in the meeting area. The use of a document camera, an interactive whiteboard, the Internet, and resources stored on digital media provides visual and interactive instructional formats that promote student engagement during whole-group mini-lessons.

In Ms. Simmons' fourth-grade whole-group meeting area, she reviews previous writing skills and demonstrates her current mini-lesson. After modeling, students engage in conversations that focus specifically on the writing skill. She expects all students, including those identified as students with special needs and English language learners, to participate in this "oral rehearsal" time. During these conversations, because of the close proximity of students, Ms. Simmons can listen in on several pair conversations and jot down her observations, and also assist and motivate when necessary. During these few minutes, students are engaged, focused, and attentive because they know Ms. Simmons shares some of her observations with direct comments from students, providing accolades and encouragement. These whole-group expectations and routines are demonstrated, practiced, and charted beginning on Day 1 of the school year (see Figure 1.3).

Figure 1.3 Sample Photos from Ms. Simmons' Class

In a whole-group demonstration, Ms. Simmons uses a vocabulary strategy to build an alphabet word chart titled The Brain, Our Nervous System to support word choice. The chart serves as a word bank as students develop their nonfiction writing.

Ms. Simmons listens and records observations as students consider additional information to include on the class chart.

Writing Desks

Picture this: a mini-lesson is complete, and students head off to their desks to work on their individual projects. The atmosphere is like a beehive, busy and active, yet productive. Mia, Garth, and Emily edit their drafts, trading papers, using their editing pens to carefully search and mark, using CUPS (Capitalization, Usage of grammar, Punctuation, Spelling) as their guide. Juan and Maria work on laptops preparing their writing for publication and providing guidance to each other. Li and Robert sit shoulder-to-shoulder in a peer conference, reading their writing pieces to each other and listening for details. Other students are at their seats engaged in meaningful conversation about their writing, exploring mentor texts, moving their pencils steadily across the page. Mrs. Rome, the teacher, is moving around, observing, conferring, and recording notes on work ethic, self-monitoring, writing progress, and intellectual aggressiveness.

This atmosphere of collaboration, supporting, and sharing is created by developing routines for writer's workshop, but it is also greatly enabled by the arrangement of student desks or tables into clustered pods consisting of four or five students. Pods are arranged so that students are face-to-face with a partner or partnered side-by-side in a group of four. Students are grouped based on academic readiness, language acquisition, behavior, personality, and social and emotional maturity. All levels of ability are included in each pod. Through observations and conversations, you will begin to know your learners and can easily make adjustments to avoid matching students with personality conflicts or different learning styles. Plan ahead! This may be the most important consideration when building a classroom-management plan. When making seating changes, remember to give students time to adjust to their new neighbors and environment. During our classroom visits, we have noticed in some upper grades that teachers use a U-shaped desk arrangement in two rows when tables and space are limited. This also allows for whole-group instruction as well as peer collaboration and easy movement for both the teacher and students.

Support student engagement and motivation by also including writing spaces around the room. These may be open to any student, designated for specific work, or assigned to a specific pod of students for the day. The area can be as simple as a small rug, a few pillows, or more refined with beanbags, directors' chairs, a yoga mat, or even a small sofa. Specific work areas might include a publishing center or a conferencing area. These mini seating areas provide students the opportunity to be away from their seats for a bit. As teachers, we have very few opportunities to sit ourselves, and we often forget that students are sitting for a large part of their day. Common sense tells us students are more attentive and productive when in a safe and comfortable environment. Figure 1.4 shows classroom setup examples for this process.

Figure 1.4 Examples of Classroom Setups

After completing a mini-lesson, students return to pods to practice their mini-lesson in student notebooks. Then they move into their writing folder and begin their individual writing projects.

Book boxes with appropriate mentor texts, as well as other resources, are provided on the writing desk, and serve as a reminder that rigor is expected and materials are available.

Individual, Peer, and Group Conference Areas

> "As a classroom teacher, you have limited space within which to organize the materials and activities essential for instruction."
>
> —Irene Fountas and Gay Su Pinnell (2001, 91)

Ms. Simmons teaches both fourth- and fifth-grade writing. She routinely arranges areas for collaboration in individual (teacher-to-student) conferences, peer (student-to-student) conferences, and small-group conferences for guided writing and writing enrichment group meetings. This organizational structure developed over time as she became more confident in her conferencing skills and students became accustomed to the routines of writer's workshop. Each of these conference styles has one important goal in common—to build confident, independent writers who are capable of critiquing and improving their personal writing. The conference process is discussed in more detail in Chapter 2.

Individual conferences can take place in just about any area of the classroom. Some teachers prefer pulling up a chair next to a student at their desk or table, thus causing little disruption (see Figure 1.5). Others meet individual students at a small table, on the carpet area, or even in the writing center. What is important is to meet students at their eye level so that they feel you next to them, supporting and guiding them through the conferencing process.

Figure 1.5 Teacher-to-Student Conferences

The teacher meets the student at his table to provide individual conference time. After he reads his text, she points out his use of descriptive words and records his achievement in her conference log.

Peer conferences can take place at students' desks, tables, or other designated areas around the room. They provide students opportunities to give constructive feedback to others and develop confidence during this sharing process, as shown in Figure 1.6. Teachers value this interactive talk time because it is essential that students receive constructive feedback to grow as writers. Magnetic name cards are kept in a basket so that students can display their card to request a peer conference. Once the two students are finished, they remove their names from the board and return them to the basket.

Figure 1.6 Sharing Writing Together

Students can affirm things they like and wonder about when sharing writing by simply teaching and providing lead-in stems such as, "I really like the way you…" and, "I wonder…."

Posted in an area, you might find directions to guide students as well as sentence stems and questions like those listed in Figure 1.7 to help students engage in the peer-conference process. With your students, develop and then model directions and sets of questions based on their developmental writing level.

Figure 1.7 Sample Peer Conference Anchor Chart

1-2-3 Peer Conference Chart

1. **Read and Listen** to your partner's writing.

2. **Compliment** (What did your partner do that good writers do?)

   - I really like the way you ...
   - What I like best about your story is ...
   - I like the way you added this detail to let the reader know ...

3. **Comment and Question** (What will make this writing better?)

   - What part are you worried about in your writing today?
   - I'm confused about this part. How can we fix it?
   - Would you like to work together to (improve _____; add details; check vocabulary; review your transitions; check spelling)?

Other questions or comments may apply, but as writers, students should leave the peer- or teacher-conferencing area with a sense of their growth as writers. Peer conferences are most successful when procedures are frequently modeled, guidelines are specific, and peer conference forms are available for support.

As we visit classrooms, we note conference areas that reflect what works best for that particular teacher with that specific group of students. For example, while visiting Ms. Judy's first-grade classroom last year, we observed Ms. Judy and Leim sitting side-by-side at his table holding an individual conference, two other students sharing their writing on the carpet with a conferencing checklist, and a student teacher modeling and guiding four other students at a small table. When visiting this year, Ms. Judy had one student at a small table and explained that this class was not quite ready for peer conferences and that she did not have a student teacher for additional support. This year, she was holding more small-group conferences along with individual-student conferences, as shown in Figure 1.8. Being willing to make adjustments and modifications is important to meet the needs of your students during writer's workshop.

Figure 1.8 Group Conference Area

The teacher invites students to her small-group table. First, she identifies and praises each student for a writing accomplishment. Then she focuses her attention on the similar and common writing needs of this group of young writers.

Materials Needed to Achieve Success

"Although students will do most of their writing in their individual space, they will need an area where writing materials are organized and easily accessible."
—Irene Fountas and Gay Su Pinnell (2001, 93)

A well-designed classroom with easy access and organization of materials can be created using inexpensive shelves, baskets, and tubs. Taking the time to teach and model procedures for using and organizing materials allows more time for actual student writing later. Decide where materials will be stored in your classroom. For example, student folders and notebooks may be stored at student desks or perhaps in colorful bins by table clusters, allowing pod leaders to easily and quickly get materials for their group. Paper, pencils, markers, scissors, glue, and other materials also need a specific space to help students become independent writers. Labeling assures student awareness of where materials and resources are as well as where they should be returned. Adding small pictures with labels supports younger students as well as English language learners. When considering writing materials and organizational tools, be mindful of the value and importance of each item and how it will directly affect the writing achievement of your students. In other words, is it necessary? Here we share materials we find valuable during our writing workshops.

Student Writing Folders

Each student uses a two-pocket, three-prong folder with plastic sleeve inserts. To organize the folder, place a green dot on the left inside pocket, which indicates work is in progress. On the right-side back pocket, add a red dot, which notes that the work is complete. Older students can write *In progress* and *Completed* on their pockets. Plastic sleeve inserts provide space for grade-level-specific resources such as alphabet charts, color and number word lists, sight word lists, long and short vowel pictures and words, examples of vowel teams, personal dictionaries, lists of adjectives, parts of speech, and grammar rules (see Figures 1.9, 1.10, and 1.11). The sleeves allow resources to be updated based on the student progress, mini-lesson focus, and individual student needs. The folder may also include forms that are personalized throughout the year by the student such as a list of topics for writing, a personal word wall, and an action word list. A variety of charts and forms are available in resources such as *Getting to the Core of Writing Series, Grades K–6* (Gentry, McNeel, and Wallace-Nesler 2012 a–f, 2013 g).

Figure 1.9 Sample Vowel Word List

Vowel Word List

Short A	Short E	Short I	Short O	Short U
add	bed	big	box	bug
ant	beg	did	dog	bus
apple	egg	dig	dot	but
ax	elk	drip	fox	drum
cat	elm	fish	frog	fun
dad	get	fit	hop	gum
fast	hen	inch	hot	hug
flag	leg	ink	log	hum
glad	men	kid	mom	rub
had	nest	lid	not	rug
man	pet	lip	on	run
pan	red	milk	pop	sun
rat	sled	mix	sock	tub
sad	ten	pig	stop	up
tag	wet	sit	top	us

Short/Long A	Short/Long E	Short/Long I	Short/Long O	Short/Long U
can/cane	pet/Pete	dim/dime	cop/cope	cub/cube
cap/cape		fin/fine	glob/globe	cut/cute
fad/fade		kit/kite	hop/hope	hug/huge
hat/hate		rid/ride	pop/pope	tub/tube
mad/made		rip/ripe	slop/slope	
pol/pole		slid/slide		
Sam/same		slim/slime		
tap/tape		Tim/time		
		twin/twine		

Long A	Long E	Long I	Long O	Long U
ape	feet	dime	bone	cute
cake	he	ice	broke	flute
date	me	like	cone	fuse
face	see	shine	drove	June
grapes	she	side	rope	rude
make	tree	size	smoke	rule
shake	bee	smile	stove	tune
skate	we	white	woke	use

(Gentry, McNeel, and Wallace-Nesler 2012 b)

Figure 1.10 Sample Vowel Teams Chart

Vowel Teams Chart

CVCe	CVCe	CVCe	CVCe	ai
cave	kite	nose	mule	rain
behave	disguise	oppose	confuse	complain
mistake	empire	pose	dispute	detain
rave	require	devote	accuse	obtain

ay	ea	ee	oa	oe
hay	eagle	cheese	boat	toe
display	league	indeed	loaves	foe
payable	meager	feeble	approach	woeful
repayment	beagle	sleet	float	doe

ie	ue	au	aw	ew
tie	glue	sauce	hawk	news
diet	tissue	author	yawn	crew
belie	rescue	sausage	drawing	screw
quiet	Tuesday	automatic	awkward	renew

(Gentry, McNeel, and Wallace-Nesler 2012 c–f; 2013 g)

Figure 1.11 Sample Sight Word List

Fry Sight Word List

First 100

a	before	get	I	me	out	there	when
about	boy	give	if	much	put	they	which
after	but	go	in	my	said	this	who
again	by	good	is	new	see	three	will
all	can	had	it	no	she	to	with
an	come	has	just	not	so	two	work
and	day	have	know	of	some	up	would
any	did	he	like	old	take	us	you
are	do	her	little	on	that	very	your
as	down	here	long	one	the	was	
at	eat	him	make	or	there	we	
be	four	his	man	other	them	were	
been	from	how	many	our	then	what	

Second 100

also	box	five	leave	name	pretty	stand	use
am	bring	found	left	near	ran	such	want
another	call	four	let	never	read	sure	way
away	came	friend	live	next	red	tell	where
back	color	girl	look	night	right	than	while
ball	could	got	made	only	run	these	white
because	dear	hand	may	open	saw	thing	wish
best	each	high	men	over	say	think	why
better	ear	home	more	own	school	too	year
big	end	house	morning	people	seem	tree	
black	far	into	most	play	shall	under	
book	find	kind	mother	please	should	until	
both	first	last	must	present	soon	upon	

Third 100

along	clothes	eyes	green	letter	ride	small	walk
always	coat	face	grow	longer	round	start	warm
anything	cold	fall	hat	light	same	stop	wash
around	cut	fast	happy	love	sat	ten	water
ask	didn't	fat	hard	money	second	thank	woman
ate	does	fine	head	myself	set	third	write
bed	dog	fire	hear	now	seven	those	yellow
brown	don't	fly	help	o'clock	show	though	yes
buy	door	food	hold	off	sing	today	yesterday
car	dress	full	hope	once	sister	took	
carry	early	funny	hot	order	sit	town	
clean	eight	gave	jump	pair	six	try	
close	every	goes	keep	part	sleep	turn	

(Gentry, McNeel, and Wallace-Nesler 2012 d–f; 2013 g)

Student Notebooks (Grades 3+)

The student notebook is an essential tool in writer's workshop from third grade and up. The use of a composition notebook that students grow to value and use as a resource throughout the year is recommended. The type of notebook—composition, binder, or spiral bound—should be a decision made based on what works for your teaching and management styles. Storing notebooks in bins, on desks, or nearby shelves with easy access for students prompts greater use of this valuable resource.

Many teachers have students decorate and personalize their writer's notebook, as shown in Figure 1.12. The notebook should contain entries that support students with writing skills connected to daily mini-lessons, along with the student's practice of that skill or author's craft. A few examples include topic lists; a list of "brilliant beginnings" from mentor texts; a list of describing words for specific emotions; examples of simple, compound, and complex sentences; and a checklist for editing. Although students practice in their notebooks, actual drafts, revisions, and editing of writing should be stored in their writing folders.

Figure 1.12 Student Example of a Writer's Notebook

Pictured is an example of a student who has personalized her writer's notebook.

Student Showcase Portfolio Folder

Portfolios "foster independence and self-evaluation skills in students" (Duffy, Jones, and Thomas 1999, 34). The showcase portfolio folder holds writing samples that represent a student's growth and achievements as a writer. Some teachers prefer a file folder, while others prefer a small binder with plastic sleeves to insert projects like small books or brochures. We typically include the student name, school year, and a picture of the student on each folder. Each month students select writing samples from their writing folders that represent their growth as a writer. Some teachers also ask students to include a brief reflection to explain their selection, such as, "I selected this piece of writing for my portfolio because...." The teacher may also select writing samples for the portfolio to show the progress of a student's writing skills. Teachers are encouraged to store these folders where students may revisit them. It is such a delight to observe students sharing their writing from the portfolio, sometimes to assist their classmates or just for fun. Lily, a kindergarten student, once exclaimed when reviewing work from early in the year in her portfolio, "That can't be my writing! I'm a terrific writer!" Students are often amazed to see how much progress they have made. Figure 1.13 shows a sample folder.

Figure 1.13 Sample Student Showcase Portfolio

Pictured is an example of how to store the showcase portfolio folders and writer's workshop folders. These folders are economical and can be used year after year.

Writer's Tool Kit for Mini-Lessons and Individual- and Small-Group Conferences

Just as a carpenter has the right tool to perform a specific task, a writer's tool kit holds the exact tools to allow you to efficiently conduct mini-lessons and conferences. These tools serve as the resources to *show*, not just tell, about writing. Create a tool kit so it is easily carried to your group-meeting area, small-group conference area, or from table to table. Being well prepared and organized promotes successful mini-lessons and conferences. Build a tool kit throughout the year, changing and adding resources based on writing curriculum and students' writing needs. Figure 1.14 shows a variety of tools you might consider for your writer's tool kit. Figure 1.15 lists the contents that could be included in a writer's tool kit.

Figure 1.14 Sample Writer's Tool Kit

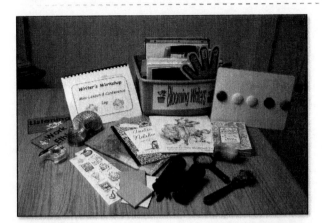

This example supports "Blooming Writers" from a primary classroom. Pictured are the contents of the kit.

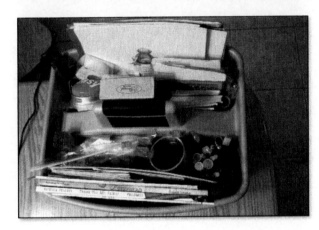

This example shows how all the materials fit into the kit for easy storage and portability.

Figure 1.15 Writer's Tool Kit Contents

Writer's Tool Kit Contents	Purpose of Contents
List of Teaching Points	• list of all skills and strategies related to the focus and genre of instruction • helps to zero in on current and/or past teaching points
Conference Prompts	• used to help facilitate conversations in student-teacher conference • examples: *Tell me about what you are trying to write today. What are some details you might add to your story to help your reader 'see' what is happening?*
Writing Samples	• appropriate for genre and developmental level of students • use teacher and student examples to demonstrate specific teaching points
Teacher's Conferring Notebook	• may include list of teaching points and conference prompts • holds conference logs and anecdotal notes of observations about student-writing behaviors, including writing strategies the student is currently exhibiting, the conference teaching point, and next steps
Your Personal Writer's Notebook	• motivates and encourages students • serves as an example during demonstrations
Examples of Children's Literature/Mentor Texts	• serve as valuable resources during modeling to generate ideas, explain structure, or demonstrate author's craft
Resource Charts	• pictures of anchor charts that have been removed to make way for new strategy charts throughout the year (primary teachers may wish to include alphabet charts, color and number charts, and name charts)
Photos and Artwork	• photos to spark interest and generate writing ideas for students in a variety of genres • authentic artwork like "Big Brother" by Dorthea Lange to show students the story within the picture
Traits of Good Writing	• for referral to the traits of quality writing when conferring with students to promote an understanding of what each represents and an understanding of the language of writing

Writer's Tool Kit Contents	Purpose of Contents
Thesaurus	• supports student understanding of parts of speech and provides synonyms to increase rigor in vocabulary
Manipulatives	• used to create visual representation and interest, such as using a Slinky® for stretching and improving sentence construction or binoculars for zooming in on details
General Supplies	• colored sticky notes: used during modeling and during conferences without marking on the student's writing • highlighters: used to call attention to specific word parts and to mark text to identify and practice lifting words, phrases, sentences, and punctuation from a mentor text • dry-erase markers and whiteboard: used to build fluency with high-frequency words from word lists, support students with spelling and formation of letters • scissors and revision strips: used to demonstrate story surgery, cutting text apart and adding in revision strips to extend, enrich, and add information • colored pencils, pens, and markers: used to demonstrate editing skills, create text during modeling, and/or make a quick sketch • index note cards: used to demonstrate the use of transition words, and to create word activities such as exploring prefixes, suffixes, root words, and word origins

Anchor Charts and Bulletin Boards

Anchor charts and bulletin boards can be valuable resources in your classroom to support student writers, or they can be "pretty pictures on the wall." We all look through the most current catalogs for materials to decorate our classrooms. With limited space and fire regulations, we must become more selective when using our wall space and decide what is essential to the learning of our students. It has been noted that students do not actually "see" items purchased and displayed but are more apt to notice and utilize anchor chart information when created together in the classroom. Think about it. We all like to see our work and feel proud that others are using it. Here are some examples of anchor charts and bulletin boards that can support student writers: invite young students to help create color and number charts; act as a scribe and have students generate examples of simple, compound, and complex sentences; create a bulletin board with examples of travel brochures, restaurant menus, letters, postcards, and articles; even résumés collected by students serve as valuable resources and exemplars. Including students in the process and displaying charts created by the class builds a sense of ownership and community within the classroom.

Mentor Texts

> "To be great writers, students must be in the company of great writers. When opportunities present themselves, we invite writers into our classroom. Since that cannot happen on a regular basis, we keep company with them through their writing!"
>
> —Judy Davis and Sharon Hill (2003, 100)

Mentor texts are those special pieces of writing that we return to and reread because they offer opportunities to teach writing skills and motivate student writing. They are texts representing a variety of genres that provide ideas, story structures, and strong examples of an author's craft. These writing pieces inspire students to take risks and try out new strategies as they become familiar with the author's craft, developing an "I wonder if I can do that?" attitude. This attitude was demonstrated by Greg, a lively fouth grader who was always moving and talking and was mischievous to a fault in and out of the classroom. Yet he was so hooked on *The Cay*, a novel written by Theodor Taylor, that he wrote his own set of short stories using the same themes: prejudice, love, and survival. Greg faithfully carried his work to and from home, and his writing folder bulged with his effort at duplicating similar stories.

Mentor texts are often quality literature such as picture books because of their amazing illustrations, interesting stories, cultural diversity, fabulous vocabulary, and connection to reading; however, mentor texts can be more than picture books. They may include an excerpt from a chapter book, a poem, or individual texts such as a newspaper column, a magazine or Internet article, cookbook, a letter to the editor, a catalogue, or a travel brochure. Katie Wood Ray (2002) encourages using a variety of texts to support writing instruction, saying, "Every single text we encounter represents a whole chunk of curriculum, a whole set of things to know about writing" (92). We select mentor texts that students can relate to with topics and strategies that challenge and excite them. Text complexity is also a consideration for mentor-text selection as students move from novice to proficient and ultimately to master readers and writers.

Recent recommendations from the national standards suggest that a greater emphasis be placed on nonfiction writing in all grade levels (National Governor's Association 2010). Along with our love and use of mentor texts in fiction and narrative writing, we must now build that same level of enthusiasm for informational text. A few nonfiction examples include the Smithsonsian Collins Series by Seymour Simon, *50 American Heroes Every Kid Should Meet* by Dennis Denenberg, and *100 True Tales from American History: The American Story* by Jennifer Armstrong. For students to become proficient in informational reading, writing, and research study, a wide range of available nonfiction texts is a must for any classroom mentor-text collection. Much of the work we do with students to inspire and to motivate them begins through lively read-alouds with much discussion, note-taking, laughter, and humor. We then pull those texts back into the discussion as we initiate our writing work in the mini-lesson phase. Just the phrase, "remember when we read …" is a signal that we're referring to a text that we want students to use as a resource. That signal might be the spark that ignites and invites students to respond to the ideas of these authors.

As novice or experienced writing teachers, you need not invest large sums of money to fill mentor-text containers with books. Use the resources in your community and school libraries, and change out mentor texts based on your units of study. Three or four great books that illustrate each trait of writing, and several books as a resource for unit study, are excellent ways to organize students to begin using principles employed by great authors. Lifting a word, phrase, sentence, or pattern boosts the quality by deliberately encouraging students to imitate the style of a mentor they respect. David, a struggling third-grade reader, used the mentor text *Swimmy* by Leo Lionni to write a host of stories about animal life in the ocean. Swimmy encouraged Leo to delve into research on animal behaviors in each layer of the ocean.

Examples of beloved literature to increase the quality of student writing should be labeled and displayed as part of your writer's workshop supplies. With the implementation of disciplinary units of study, mentor texts should also be placed in tubs and labeled so that they reflect science, social studies, history, or mathematics units. Store texts so they are easily accessible for students to examine and explore. Color coordinated dishpans make excellent containers for a variety of texts. Suggested lists of literature may be found on the Internet or in printed resources such as *Getting to the Core of Writing* (Gentry, McNeel, and Wallace-Nesler 2012 a–f, 2013 g).

Writing and Publishing Centers

Providing areas for writing and publishing centers/stations sends a message to students that you value writing and look forward to their future writing and illustrations. Like other centers or stations, it is important to establish routines, provide materials, and allow the time needed to produce successful writing projects. Model and create guidelines with your students for what to do in those areas, and clearly display those expectations.

Writing aids created by you and your students, and examples of published writing, such as an anchor chart for the parts of a letter, as well as a published letter, offer guidance and support for successful writing projects. A few suggestions to include at publishing centers/stations to encourage and motivate students to write and publish include computers, clip art, student-friendly software and websites along with a wide variety of sizes, colors, and shapes of writing paper, booklets, pencils, pens, crayons, markers, scissors, staplers, glue, tape, magazines with pictures, and scrap paper. Keep in mind to model and provide a variety of writing samples to ensure successful and proud authors.

Tips for Setting Up Your Writer's Workshop

➤ Start with a quick sketch of your classroom to gain awareness of traffic flow and movement during writer's workshop.

➤ Establish areas for whole-group instruction and small-group, peer, and individual conferences.

➤ Create clusters or pods of desks to promote writing partnerships and conversations. Use rotating team captains to perform tasks like distributing materials, notebooks, and folders as well as cleaning up the area.

- ➤ Be proactive and anticipate potential negative behaviors by modeling and creating expectations and guidelines with students and by providing praise for students who meet and exceed expectations.

- ➤ Provide materials, time, and space for student writing and publishing. We all become better writers by writing.

- ➤ Keep modeling and conferencing resources in a tool kit for easy accessibility during instruction and conferences.

- ➤ Use anchor charts, bulletin boards, and wall space wisely to display supportive writing aids.

- ➤ Use and provide access to mentor texts for exploring the author's craft.

- ➤ Teach from your feet and not your seat. To be successful, move around the room using a slight touch, gesture, or thumbs-up to encourage positive attitudes.

- ➤ Build a community of writers in which all students are included in writer's workshop. Differentiate writing instruction through small-group and individual conferences. No one is isolated for any reason because they are each a part of your community of writers.

- ➤ Ask for help and ideas from teaching colleagues. Most teachers are flattered when asked to share their expertise and are happy to mentor. We all have talents to share with one another.

Whether you are a novice or a seasoned teacher of writer's workshop, bring a positive attitude and create an environment in which students love to write. Creating an "I can" attitude as you write with your students is a sure way to create a successful community of writers in your classroom.

Reflect and Review

1. What changes can you make in your classroom to better accommodate writer's workshop?

2. Draw a sketch of how you can set up your classroom for writer's workshop. Consider the following:

   - A large area for a group meeting is essential for whole-group instruction. The group area might have a document camera, an interactive whiteboard, or a projector.

   - Materials and resources are organized by genre or content areas in tubs, baskets, or containers.

   - Arrange the furniture to accommodate small groupings of students working cooperatively. Consider arranging your room into groups of four. Place the small-group table where you have full view of all students.

   - Visualize the classroom in action. Consider your overall physical setup and check the room for workspace, physical comfort, and accessibility of writing materials and resources.

   - Consider how you will use wall space for displaying anchor charts and student work.

   - Create storage of writer's folders and writer's notebooks that is easily accessible for students.

Chapter 2

Managing Your Writing Classroom

"Make excellent management a priority. Better classroom managers are more likely to teach for meaning and less likely to have mastery of discrete skills as their main instructional goal."

—Regie Routman (2005, 184)

The writer's workshop model of instruction has been around for a long time and emulates that of the craftsman and the apprentice of early ages. Like the craftsman, the teacher shares knowledge and models skills for the student. The student, like an apprentice, pays careful attention and watches closely. The apprentice practices with guidance from the craftsman, much as the student explores and practices writing skills with teacher support during conferences. The apprentice continues working on his or her skills and then shares the end product with the craftsman and friends. As students develop their writing, they also share their accomplishments. True craftsmanship is developed over time with teaching, practice, guidance, and celebrations, just as writers develop their craft through teaching, writing, guidance, sharing, and celebrating. Each student develops as a craftsman of writing if we establish a structure and routine during writer's workshop that includes a daily time for teaching, writing, conferencing, and sharing.

The Daily Schedule

"The development of children's writing from early forms to conventional forms is best achieved through substantial time devoted to writing, multiple opportunities to write across the school day, and focused instruction that builds from the writers' efforts."

—Kathy Egawa (1998)

How often do we hold a writer's workshop? Only on the days you eat! This is obviously an exaggeration, but we use this phrase to emphasize the understanding that writing is not just an add-on to fit into a few days during the week. Every day is a writing day. Not only should daily time for writer's workshop be scheduled, but time should also be spent in each content area formulating essential questions, finding sources of information, and engaging in both writing to learn and learning to write. Connie Dierking and Sherra Jones, authors of *Growing Up Writing* (2003) state, "When working under the structure of a daily writer's workshop, emergent and beginning writers will astound their audiences. Their accomplishments have no limits: enjoy their stories, applaud their efforts. Let them write, every day. The payoff is priceless (2–3)." The same can be said for students at any developmental stage of writing.

Like Calkins (1994), Portalupi and Fletcher (1998), and Ray and Laminack (2001), our writer's workshop comprises three components:

Time to Teach: The teacher, or sometimes a student, models a brief, explicit mini-lesson with the whole class that focuses on a specific writing skill or author's craft.

Time to Write and Confer: Students engage in writing and illustrating projects and individual, small-group, and peer conferences are held. This is the largest block of time during the workshop.

Time to Share: Students share their writing and reflect on their needs and progress. Often neglected for lack of time, sharing provides accountability, reflection, and motivation.

Suggested times for each component are shown in Figure 2.1. Be mindful that these times should reflect the time of year, developmental level of your students, and mini-lesson. What is most important is for students to have some writing time every day.

Figure 2.1 Writer's Workshop At-a-Glance

Component	Suggested Time
Mini-Lesson	5–15 Minutes
Writing and Conferencing	15–30 Minutes*
Sharing	5–15 Minutes

*Kindergarten and first-grade students may begin with as little as 5–10 minutes until they build up their writing stamina. In the same way, older students may extend their time beyond 30 minutes based on stamina, projects, and motivation.

In our series, *Getting to the Core of Writing K–6* (2012 a–f and 2013 g), we follow this format for managing the daily writer's workshop, which can easily include cross-curricular writing activities as well. For example, a fourth-grade classroom might study a unit on geology in science. During a scheduled writer's workshop, students may write poetry about rocks, compose letters to geologists, generate jingles to familiar tunes, create informational alphabet books, or prepare reports with summarized information collected on a nature walk. Within the structured format of the workshop, tap into your students' potential and expect each one to engage in writing activities of their choosing.

When we commit to a daily writing routine, students recognize the value that we as teachers place on writing, and they in turn develop an appreciation and understanding of the value of writing in their lives. In Ms. Weber's fourth-grade classroom, Serena complained because writer's workshop was interrupted with an unscheduled assembly: "What do you mean, we have to give up writer's workshop? I'm in the middle of a poetry project!" In the ideal implementation, writer's workshop becomes a schoolwide initiative, where students move from class to class and grade to grade with the familiar language, expectations, and routines. The school and all stakeholders view writing as an essential element necessary for becoming successful.

Time to Teach: The Mini-Lesson

One essential component of your writer's workshop is delivering effective mini-lessons that challenge and elevate students' writing abilities. Talking about writers, studying other writers, and practicing the craft of writing gives students an undeniable gift of "being an author." Mini-lessons are brief and taught during the first 5–15 minutes of daily writer's workshop in the whole-group meeting area. It may be a single lesson or a sequence of lessons with one instructional focus based on each student's needs identified during observations, conferences, and assessments. While the focus of the mini-lesson may change each day, the mini-lesson routine remains constant. Building routines in any instruction yields smooth transitions between activities and fewer opportunities for distractions. The mini-lessons used in writer's workshop are grouped into three categories (Calkins 1994; Dorn and Soffos 2001; Fountas and Pinnell 2001).

- management (what we do)
- process and content (how and what we write)
- craft (how we connect)

Management

These mini-lessons teach students procedures and guidelines necessary for creating an efficient and productive workshop. Procedures and guidelines may include gathering for writer's workshop, where to sit during whole-group meetings, where to get materials, how to partner-talk and listen, where to keep their writing folders, how to use the writer's notebook, and how to use an editing checklist.

Process and Content

This category encompasses the foundational conventions of writing, such as sentence structure, grammar, and punctuation. Also included are mini-lessons focused on creating content, like gathering and creating ideas for writing, staying on topic, creating a plan for writing, organizing information, using precise words, and characteristics of narrative or informational writing.

Craft

Craft mini-lessons to give students an understanding of the quality writing characteristics authors use to connect to their readers. Examples of craft mini-lessons that can elevate students' writing might include show, don't tell, the power of three, using a repeating line/phrase, brilliant beginnings/leads, creating circle endings, and using similes and sensory details.

The Struture of a Mini-Lesson

When planning the content for mini-lessons, connect the teaching focus to the needs of the majority of students so that all students are engaged participants during the mini-lesson. Address specific needs through differentiated instruction during individual and small-group conferences. Regardless of their writing ability, students practice listening and speaking skills, benefit from explicit focused instruction, and become familiar with the language of writing. Like the predictable components of writer's workshop, the mini-lesson flows in an organized structure to support student learning. We suggest the following mini-lesson structure:

- **Thinking About Writing:** Provide a brief explanation of what students will be learning and how it relates to previous learning, other literacy or subject content, and/or the world around them.

- **Teaching:** "I will show you" clearly reveals the intention of this portion of a writing lesson. It explicitly states the focus of the mini-lesson and how it supports the student as a writer now and forever. Next is a demonstration, the most powerful form of teaching, especially when it includes a model of the intended writing. As a writer, share an example by thinking aloud and sharing each step of the intended strategy. The selected topic is the writing skill, strategy, or craft that will elevate the writing level of students.

- **Engaging:** Expect students to engage in the practice of talking about strategies they will apply in their writing. Typically, students form a partnership and engage in an "oral rehearsal" before trying out the skill during writing-practice time. The talk time is short, intense, and focused. Monitor time, observe, and praise by sharing examples of good practice through positive, supportive comments.

- **Applying:** We want students to understand the importance of the teaching so that the intention of the lesson is always present. Restate the mini-lesson focus to remind students not only to explore this new writing concept today but also to add it to their collection of writing tools. Students should head off to their writing work with energy, enthusiasm, and an "I can do that!" attitude.

Time to Write and Confer

One of the most valued gifts we can give young writers is time to write, explore, and practice writing skills, strategies, and author's crafts. Students learn by doing. They gain confidence as writers by being engaged in authentic writing. Students want to write. They begin by scribbling as toddlers. On the first day of school, they often expect to be able to read and write. Not only does building writing stamina require grit, consistency, work ethic, drive, and resilience, but it also supports, provides guidance, and affirms.

Successful conferencing is an engaging conversation with the student doing the majority of the talking. Students soon recognize conferences as a predictable and scheduled part of writer's workshop. Circulate around the room, moving table to table or desk to desk. You may prefer a small conference table to hold one-on-one conferences or possibly small guided-writing groups.

"Observe, praise, guide!" is our mantra for conferring. Say it to yourself as you approach a student writer, and it will keep you on track in this powerful component of writer's workshop as you help the writer make connections to what you have taught. Lucy Calkins (2003) affirms the importance of conferring for writers: "Conferring is the heart of the writing workshop. Indeed, it is the very heart of teaching writing itself. When it is done well, it can change the course of a writing life forever" (viii). Writing conferences are most successful when they occur as a conversation between two writers just "talking about writing." It is a time to value students as writers, to differentiate instruction, to teach or reinforce new strategies, and to gather information for forming instructional decisions. Anderson (2001) notes that a conference conversation basically includes two parts: conversation based upon the child's current writing and conversation based on what will help the child become a better writer. Katie Wood Ray and Lester Laminack (2001) and Lucy Calkins (2003) tell us that conferring is free flowing. It is one part of the day that is a bit "unknown." Although the structure of a conference is predictable in nature, the content is determined by the response to what a student shows and tells about his or her writing. When conferring one-to-one with writers, there is no script or specific plan developed prior to the meeting.

Although a conversation between two writers, the conference structure is predictable. First, study to determine what the writer knows, what the writer is trying to learn, and what the writer needs to learn. Then provide praise, develop a teaching point, and encourage the writer to practice that teaching point. Before moving to conduct another conference, remind students to always use what was learned in future writing.

We recommend the following four phases for writing conferences: *observe*, *praise*, *guide*, and *connect*.

Observe

Use observations to build background knowledge about what the writer knows and can do independently. Use the Vygoskian concept known as zone of proximal development as you ask yourself, "What tasks is the student unable to complete without my help, but can complete with my guidance?" (Vygotsky 1978). Use probing, open-ended questioning techniques to help the writer explain ideas and feelings, gain clarity, and develop a deeper understanding of his or her work. Ask the writer:

- So, how's your writing going today?
- Can you tell me about your important writing work?
- What can you tell me about your picture?

Praise

Recognize what the writer is doing correctly and what will move this student forward in his or her development as a writer. Always begin the conference with positive feedback; find something the writer is doing well. Use phrases such as "Clever you!" "What a brilliant idea!" and "That is smart writing work!" As you become more knowledgeable about the developmental phases of writers and shape your own understanding of quality writing instruction, praise will become more powerful, authentic, and sophisticated. Suggestions to get started include:

- Your setting sounds just like . . . (insert an author's name and book title here, e.g., Jane Yolen's from *Owl Moon*).

- You've used descriptions that create an excellent image!

- You must be so proud of how you used your great work ethic.

- Your pencil was quickly moving across the paper, and look at what you've already accomplished!

- Your character description is very detailed. I can really picture (him/her) in my head!

Remind students of the exact language or features they have used effectively and tell them to always use that in their writing.

Guide

Through your observations, determine a teaching point to move the student toward independence and decide how to demonstrate and teach it. Selecting a teaching point can be daunting as we analyze a writer's work. Teachers often ask, "How do you know what to work on when there are so many things?" The truth is there is no "right" answer. Use these thoughts to guide you in selecting teaching points:

- May I teach you something good writers do?

- Sometimes in my writing, I try to …

- (Pull out a mentor text for support) … Let me show you how (insert author's name here) might try that.

- Remember in our mini-lesson when we … You might try …

Coach, scaffold, and demonstrate to meet the writer's needs. The instruction includes recognition of the writer's abilities. Name and share the strategy, using demonstrations when needed. When the decision is based on a previously taught mini-lesson, writers make additional connections and greater success is achieved. Using explicit language, state what the student will learn, and meet eye to eye at their level. Offering support while the writer practices the strategy increases the chance for success. Once the writer is engaged in practice, confer with another writer. Note observations in writing, and leave the writer with the expectations that "when I return, I expect to see…." Always return briefly to provide specific feedback relative to your expectations.

Connect

Link the teaching point to the whole-group mini-lesson when appropriate and clearly restate the teaching point that the writer practiced and learned. Remind and encourage the writer to use this strategy in future writing. As students become familiar with the conference structure, ask them to share the new learning. Making connections may begin with using the following language:

- Tell your partner what you learned today as a writer. Then, share with the whole group, using a couple of examples.

- Remember, good writers always …

- How did your work connect to our mini-lesson?

Spotlight a student during writing practice time using a mini-flashlight. To do this, shine the light on a student's work which should gain the class' attention. Then announce the task or skill you wish to highlight for the rest of the class. Spotlighting requires little effort, yet it supports student writing attempts. Students need many affirmations of a job well done, and "spotlighting strategies" is the perfect opportunity to provide that praise. Use a quick comment such as, "Writers, notice how Justine has made a picture that matches the language in her text." Spotlighting writing gives recognition and validation to the writer's effort. On occasion, the spotlight strategy may be a skill or specific task you want to emphasize to writers for further understanding.

Peer Conferences

Student-led conferences are valuable to support the growth of writers. Implement peer conferencing further into the year when classroom management has been firmly established. Students are more motivated, take ownership of the workshop routines, and increase their capacity for productive language conversation. Peers can be good listeners and provide productive feedback, but structures and supportive lessons must be in place before implementation. Regie Routman (2005) notes that "students can be used as peer editors to improve mechanics and overall fluency" (220). However, feedback on organization and craft requires more sophisticated knowledge and might be best provided by the teacher.

We often demonstrate a peer conferring session using a "Fish Bowl" strategy to show what productive talk should look like and sound like. Students form a circle in the whole-group meeting area. Calling up a student who feels comfortable and can engage in a lively conversation, the teacher and student each hold a piece of their writing. With the class listening in (younger students) or taking notes (older students), the fish in the bowl (teacher and student) begin one at a time to read their text and engage in questioning strategies and problem-solving skills. Keep it simple! When done well, getting feedback from peers about writing can change the course of student writing and lift the quality of your writer's workshop. Figure 2.2 provides sample questions that students can ask each other during peer conferencing.

Figure 2.2 Sample Peer Conferencing Questions

(Gentry, McNeel, and Wallace-Nesler 2012 d–f; 2013 g)

Small-Group Conferences

Small-group conferences should be treated like guided writing groups, similar to guided reading groups and providing opportunities for differentiated writing instruction. The method of instruction resembles the individual conference: observe, praise, guide, and connect. Groups are selected based on similar needs identified from observations during the whole-group mini-lessons, sharing, and data from writing samples as well as requirements from local and state writing curriculums. Scheduling small-group conferences provides more time to work closely with all students and opportunities to build an awareness of both their strengths and struggles in writing. The smaller group time enhances the intensity of instruction by targeting specific skills and increasing instructional time. Other advantages of the small group are extra modeling and demonstration and more time for practicing the writing skill with explicit feedback. Teachers often report that small-group conferences enrich their students' writing and elevate writing scores on assessments. For additional information on materials to be used in this setting, refer to the Writer's Tool Kit in Chapter 1.

Fourth-grade teacher, Ms. Simmons, modeled a mini-lesson on transition words using the interactive whiteboard with her own piece of writing and then directed students to use transition words entered in their notebooks. After students settled into their writing task, Ms. Simmons quickly asked six students to join her with their notebooks at the small-group table. She shared a variety of transition word cards and supported students as they sorted them into categories. As students reread their writing, they chose a transition word card to fit and lift their level of writing. During this conference, she used scaffolded instruction to guide students through their writing work and monitored progress by taking notes in her conference log. Figure 2.3 shows this small-group conference.

Figure 2.3 Small-Group Conference

Ms. Simmons holds a small-group conference to improve student writing and test-taking strategies by demonstrating how to embed organizational structures.

Time to Share

> "As I've begun to conduct share sessions as discussions, I've been dazzled by the ways in which these meetings have the capacity to lift energy, build morale, encourage participation, and most of all instruct."
>
> —Leah Mermelstein (2007, 8)

Sharing is the final component of writer's workshop. Sharing provides students opportunities to converse, explain, question, and give feedback to their group or partner. Students share portions of their writing relating to the day's mini-lesson focus. Be consistent, yet group in a variety of ways to keep students motivated and eager to discuss and reread their writing. Use only three seconds to move students into their grouping. Utilize a phrase such as, "Writers! Take three seconds and move to your writing partner. Now, take some time to share your important writing work today. When you are finished, move into a quad and share your best sentence." Providing consistent sharing time not only holds students accountable during writer's workshop, but it also gives them credibility and recognition as writers.

Planning time for sharing is crucial as an opportunity to provide further teaching points. In general, specific procedures are followed when guiding sharing sessions. In a whole-group share, in which students take the "author's chair," observe and select students who exhibit writing that echoes the point of the mini-lesson or recognize specific accomplishments of the writers. Decisions based on roving conferences, small-group enrichment, and guided writing groups provide the perfect venue for selecting a text for discussion and questioning. No matter the grade level of students, expect comments and questions during sharing reflections of writing. The level of contributions to discussions is elevated by teacher demonstrations that model expected guidelines for sharing. Be careful to set limits during whole-group share. Make a note of the number of students sharing and the allotted time.

Mrs. Hammel, a second-grade teacher, conducted a great writing session. Writing was productive, students were energetic, and the enthusiasm was palpable. From our observations, we noted three students who shared their writing to provide examples that would benefit the class. However, after visiting other scheduled classes and later passing by her classroom again, we noticed that Mrs. Hammel found the sharing so significant that she allowed everyone in the class to share, but it took way too much time. Organizing a partner share would have made this much more productive.

Often students find a partner share less intimidating and feel empowered because they have a consistent audience. This sharing is useful for lifting the level of conversation and for building language competencies. Partner shares can be easily moved into a small-group share by having two sets of partners join together.

You might be wondering how you can organize for different shares. Quite simply, practice makes perfect. During the mini-lesson, explicitly state, "Today, I will show you how to meet with your classmates to share." You might be picturing chaos in your head—not the case if you carefully plan, model, and demonstrate exactly how you want it to look and feel. It never fails! Direct students to move quickly and quietly by the time you count to three. Repeat this process until you have reached automaticity. Once expectations have been achieved with partner routines, move students into small groups, using the same language and having two sets of partners to create a small sharing group. The secret is to "show, not tell" as expectations are modeled. Gradually, as students learn to self-monitor their own behavior, expect them to move forward, validating the work of their peers. Thus re-teaching is often not needed as frequently.

Tips for Productive Sharing Time

➤ Model, model, model.

➤ Practice, practice, practice to build routines.

➤ Decide whether to assign partnerships or randomly partner depending on the personality of your class.

➤ Have partners stand shoulder-to-shoulder, facing the same direction while reading each other's writing.

➤ Have partners maintain expected listening behaviors as practiced in classroom routines.

➤ Have partners provide reflection and feedback using language that has been practiced.

➤ Direct small groups to form, or as suggested previously, move partners into teams of four.

➤ Have small groups stand in a circle or sit in a circle.

The teacher's role is to listen in, problem solve, negotiate, and make certain that no member of the team is monopolizing the conversation. Believe in students' capacity to share and value one another's work and in the power of writing to transform their world. Successful writing has the power to change the lives of students forever. For evidence, we need only to look back at Isaiah, a fourth grader with an infectious grin and a love of writing. Isaiah was transformed inside and outside the classroom when he was supported as a struggling writer. "You are working with us today?" he inquired with eager anticipation after the turnaround. He became a writer under our apprenticeship. Much of his success grew out of valuing and sharing his work. Not only was Isaiah able to write successfully about topics of his own choice, but he also could transfer that success to the reality of prompted writing. He began to experience Angelillo's goal: "It is essential to establish a literacy community that focuses on teaching students to write well for any occasion" (Angelillo 2005, 7).

Fast forward two years later. Isaiah popped out of his dad's car to pick up a sibling. He hugged his former writing teacher, smiled, and gave a reminder that his writing skills were still intact: he was doing well in his local middle school. Writing transformed the life of Isaiah. The secret was writing daily, building his confidence, sharing, and a celebration of risk taking.

Routines

In our experience, when teachers ask for support because their writer's workshop is just not working, it is almost always a lack of management, procedures, and expectations, not the actual writing instruction. Classroom and instructional management styles are influenced by past teachers, observations of fellow colleagues and consultants, knowledge acquired from readings and workshops, and the unique personalities. We are not, and will never be, cookie-cutter teachers, but we can establish similar, specific routines to create an environment where students want and love to write.

The most important word that comes to mind when thinking about routines is *consistency*. Be consistent so that you and your students have a clear understanding of the expectations and guidelines for writer's workshop. When introducing routines, assume nothing; model everything. We cannot assume students already know or will remember exactly what to do after only being told once (or twice, or even three times). Expect to spend the opening of the school year demonstrating and practicing routines. Keep in mind that the routines established in the classroom guide students in becoming independent, productive, responsible, and caring classmates.

As routines are built for each component of writer's workshop, create a cumulative class anchor chart to reinforce expected behaviors. Decide together what writer's workshop, or your classroom in general, should look like, sound like, and feel like. Take responsibility for communicating and maintaining an atmosphere of learning that is both comfortable and productive for you and your students. Consider the anchor charts in Figures 2.4, 2.5, and 2.6 as examples of creating guidelines with students.

Figure 2.4 Sample Looks Like, Sounds Like, Feels Like Anchor Chart

Sample Looks Like, Sounds Like, Feels Like Anchor Chart

Our Writer's Workshop...

Looks Like	Sounds Like	Feels Like
· Pencils, all supplies ready	· Buzz, hum, beehive	· Comfortable, natural, happy
· Journals/folders/notebooks	· Two-inch voices	· Nonthreatening, risk taking
· Mentor texts available	· Conversation/oral language	· Purposeful
· Anchor charts	· Quiet during thinking and teaching phase	· Successful
· Author's chair	· "Hum" when sharing with partners, triads, quads	· Confident
· Partners/small groups	· Busy	· Excited
· Smiling faces	· Students making decisions	· Relaxed
· Writing tool kits	· Learning is happening	· Proud
· Student engagement	· Questioning	· Comfortable sharing thoughts
· Vocabulary list	· Writing is individualized/differentiated	· "I can" attitude
· Writing prompts		
· Turn and talk		
· Productive		
· Organized		
· Writing		
· Busy		

(Gentry, McNeel, and Wallace-Nesler 2012 a–f; 2013 g)

Figure 2.5 Sample Guidelines for Writer's Workshop

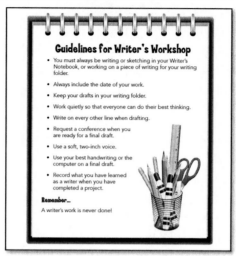

Guidelines for Writer's Workshop

- You must always be writing or sketching in your Writer's Notebook, or working on a piece of writing for your writing folder.
- Always include the date of your work.
- Keep your drafts in your writing folder.
- Work quietly so that everyone can do their best thinking.
- Write on every other line when drafting.
- Request a conference when you are ready for a final draft.
- Use a soft, two-inch voice.
- Use your best handwriting or the computer on a final draft.
- Record what you have learned as a writer when you have completed a project.

Remember...
A writer's work is never done!

(Gentry, McNeel, and Wallace-Nesler 2012 a–f; 2013 g)

Figure 2.6 Sample Partner Conversation Chart

Sample Partner Conversation Chart

- Find your partner quickly.
- Use a soft, two-inch voice.
- Make eye contact with your partner.
- Stick to the writing topic.
- Ask questions to clarify thinking.
- Make sure each partner has a turn to talk.
- Give a compliment when needed.
- Only "put-ups"—NO "put-downs."

(Gentry, McNeel, and Wallace-Nesler 2012 a–c)

Frequently Asked Questions About Management

During professional development workshops that we conduct, we have teachers place questions on a large chart known as the "parking lot." At the close of the session, we address those questions and are never surprised to find that three questions always appear on the chart.

What do I do when my student says, "I don't have anything to write about?"

Even the best of writers find themselves searching for writing ideas. Ask yourself, "Have I taught a variety of mini-lessons that focus on ideas for writing? Did we record writing ideas on an anchor chart, in our folders, or in our notebooks? Are we sharing our writing each day?" Be sure to teach mini-lessons that encourage students to make an expert list (a list of things they feel they know with expertise), or a list of favorite and interesting people and places. An "I wonder" list often lends itself to nonfiction topics for writing. Writing ideas should be displayed in the classroom, recorded in folders and/or notebooks, and always available to add new possibilities. Sharing is also a surefire winner to generate ideas for writing. Nika shared her story about going to her dad's baseball game, which reminded Alex of the time his brother slid into first base and broke his leg. Maria recalled a baseball flying through their apartment window and falling right onto the kitchen table. Your stories, your students' stories, and our favorite authors' stories all generate ideas for writing. Take the time to establish a routine of adding writing ideas to lists throughout the year.

What about students who constantly ask, "How do you spell ...?"

There are no easy answers about spelling. It should be taught explicitly in elementary school classrooms. A few suggestions to help create independent spellers are:

- Use an appropriate silent gesture with students to signal that they are not to interrupt during your time with a student (e.g., a red/green card, stop sign).

- Encourage students to record the sounds they hear when they stretch out the word.

- Check the word wall or word bank created together for a specific topic or content area.

- "Ask three then me." The student quietly checks with three other resources that may include other students, dictionaries, or a computer's spell check.

- Search for words in a writing folder and/or notebook resources.

What do I do with students who say, "I'm done! Now what do I do?"

We share the idea that there is no such thing as "finished" during writer's workshop. Teach students routines, and create options together to display on a chart. Remember to include illustrations on the chart for younger students. Teach revision and editing mini-lessons so that students can add interesting words and details as well as check for punctuation or spelling. Students may wish to add illustrations, start a new piece, pull out an older piece of writing to revise, or select writing for publication. You know you have taught routines well when you announce that writer's workshop is over for the day and students object with, "Not yet!" and "No way!"

Top Five Tips for Managing Writer's Workshop

1. Schedule writer's workshop daily

2. Model, model, model

3. Confer weekly (observe → praise → guide → connect)

4. Share, share, share using authentic praise

5. Establish and commit to routines

We are surrounded by extraordinary students just waiting for acknowledgments of their success stories. We are reminded that "Fish swim, birds fly, and people feel," famously quoted by Haim Ginott. Students want to be challenged; therefore, expectations need to extend their reach. Indeed, some of your students will be poets, authors, and successful professionals in a field of their choosing. They may not remember your classroom management techniques, but they will remember that you taught them to write.

Reflect and Review

1. What routines can you adopt to make your classroom more manageable for writer's workshop?

2. How can mini-lessons enhance your writing instruction? Consider your current instruction: what changes will you make to support writing instruction using mini-lessons?

3. How will you encourage students to engage in meaningful writing conferences with you and/or their peers?

4. Why is it important for students to share writing? How will you prepare students to respect the writing of others? What are some successful sharing techniques you have used? What are some challenges you face during sharing?

Chapter 3

Teaching Writing as a Process

"We wish to give each child regular opportunities to discover and develop his or her own variety of process and to become confident in applying it to a wide range of writing tasks."

—Donald Graves (1994, 14)

Donald Graves was the leader of a revolution in the teaching of writing and the father of the writing process as practiced in many of today's schools. Before Graves, teaching writing focused on a product. As such, teaching writing meant assigning a topic, requiring rigid outlines, imposing structures such as a five-paragraph essay, counting off for errors, and grading everything students wrote. Often the teacher was the only one reading students' papers. Today it's widely accepted that writing is best taught as a process as outlined by Donald Graves.

Graves began with three essential elements for writing process, "the child's choice of topic, the child's control of the writing, and publication for a real audience" (Walshe 1982, 14). His writing process has often been presented from a reductionist perspective as five steps: prewriting, drafting, editing, revising, and publishing. But teaching writing as a process isn't really about a five-step teaching methodology. It's about a revolution in the teaching of writing that began when Graves founded the Writing Process Laboratory at the University of New Hampshire in 1976. It would have a profound impact on the teaching of writing in the English-speaking world. Understanding why we call Graves's writing process revolutionary—a switch from product orientation to process orientation—sets the stage for understanding the five-step process.

Graves attributed much of his thinking to his collaboration with his friend Don Murray, an author, essayist, writing teacher, and fellow professor at the University of New Hampshire. They, along with Graves's students and research assistants at the Writing Process Laboratory, directed by Graves and notably including Lucy Calkins as one of its first research assistants, conducted classroom research projects that gave authority to the writing process as we know it today.

Switching from product to process changes the role of the teacher. The essential role of the process-writing teacher is to model, conference, and ask questions—not to assign, impose requirements, and grade. Graves's revolutionary concept was that all students are writers—that is to say, all students have something to say, and they can make meaning on paper even from a very early age. It might start with drawing pictures from their imagination and scribbling. It's a creativity process. The inspiration and motivation to write, Graves believed, must come from the child and satisfy an innate human drive to speak out and create meaning (as cited in Walshe 1982). When teaching writing as a process, teachers invite students to write, respond to their ideas, and foster their development.

Writing, then, is not a set of skills to be taught. It's a craft to be learned. So, like the artist or potter who learns in studios or workshops, the craft of writing is taught in a workshop where the student learns to write under the tutorship and guidance of a writing teacher who is the master craftsman, modeling and practicing the craft alongside the student.

Ownership is at the core of teaching the writing process—the belief that the student, not the teacher, owns the piece. Time to compose, trust, respect, and ownership are guiding principles for process writing. For example, Graves believed choice of topic should be owned by the student. As he famously said, "When people own a place, they look after it; but when it belongs to someone else, they couldn't care less. It's this way with writing" (Walshe 1982, 9). Respecting ownership in process-writing classrooms can be subtle. For example, consider writing comments on sticky notes and never on the students' texts. We recommend that you always keep sticky notes in your writer's tool kit and ask, "May I show you something?" or "May I make a suggestion that may help you as a writer?" Then write it on a sticky note and attach it to the paper.

The process-writing principles of choice of topic, ownership, writing for a real audience, time for composing, and feedback through conferencing are indeed revolutionary. These principles, along with believing in Graves's notion that "Children want to write," have led to the basic methodology of the writer's workshop including the five-step writing process.

The Five-Step Writing Process

Teaching writing in the classroom has shifted from focus on products to studying the processes associated with how writers write (Dyson and Freedman 1990). The five-step writing process is the following cycle of craft: pre-writing, drafting, revising, editing, and publishing. Think of this five-step process as the engine driving your writer's workshop where you model and teach writing as you conduct mini-lessons, send students off to write, continue to teach and monitor progress by conferring with individuals and small groups, and ultimately create a community where all writers collaborate and share. Students will be at various stages in the process when directed to write. Some may be prewriting, others may be drafting, and a small group may be peer editing, yet everyone understands the process and is engaged with one of its stages. It's important to note that as writers become more sophisticated, steps in the writing process become recursive and the cycle becomes less rigid. During revision, for example, a piece may take a completely different course requiring a new draft, that is to say, the first draft becomes the prewriting for the second draft. Another recursive example is when students edit whatever they are working on currently for spelling, looking for a particular spelling pattern they are studying in the weekly spelling unit, even though they aren't ready to edit the completed piece. Keeping this information in mind, let's look at each of the five steps in more detail.

Step 1: Prewriting

Prewriting involves decision making, rehearsal, and perhaps putting down a plan. It's when writers generate ideas, make decisions regarding the genre or type of piece they plan to write, rehearse how a piece might develop, and begin to put their thoughts in order. Once students understand the concept of prewriting, rehearsal can take place out of the classroom as they get an idea for writing when watching a favorite TV show, riding their bikes, sitting on the bus to school, listening to a snippet of conversation, or seeing something impressionable.

With beginners, prewriting often starts with a drawing. Drawing spawns great writing topics and reveals the following information about beginning writers:

- what's on their mind

- what they know about

- what they are interested in

- what makes an impression on them

- what they like or dislike

- what they feel strongly about

- what they might like to write

In Kindergarten, prewriting might be playing in "The Restaurant Center" where students take roles such as owner, cook, waiter, or patron and pretend to read a menu, order something, pay the check, and add a tip. Play as prewriting provides numerous opportunities for very young students to write. Talk is important for prewriting. Sometimes prewriting is talk written down. Prewriting can also spring from thinking about the senses: touch, taste, sound, sight, and smell.

Prewriting lessons sometimes follow a concrete graphic organizer or template. Teachers often introduce graphic organizers to help students in the prewriting phase. In the lesson, they model how they might use a particular prewriting graphic organizer and show a teacher-generated piece of writing that was developed from the graphic organizer before students do the same on their own. Prewriting graphic organizers can also help students narrow the topic. Some popular graphic organizers used for prewriting are found in Chapter 6.

Figure 3.1 shows an example of a pre-writing graphic organizer used for narrowing the topic. Our analogy of a watermelon to seed may be used to help writers narrow a broad topic such as *going to Grandma's house*, to just the house, then just the kitchen, to the "seed story." In this case, it's baking cookies with Grandma.

Figure 3.1 Sample Prewriting Organizer

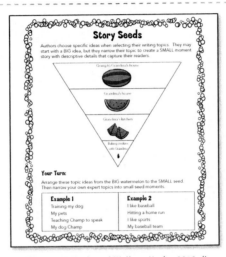

(Gentry, McNeel, and Wallace-Nesler 2012 d)

The Hand Plan in Figure 3.2 can be adapted in prewriting at different grade levels for different purposes, addressing increasing levels of sophistication. We introduce a prewriting Hand Plan for first or second graders featuring topic, detail, detail, detail, detail, and wrap-up. It can later be adapted for any five-point construction such as planning a story with introduction, the problem, the big event, the resolution, and the ending. It can also be used for the classic six-point paragraph essay: introduction with thesis statement, first strongest argument, second strongest argument, third strongest argument, fourth strongest argument, and concluding paragraph echoing the preceding material.

Figure 3.2 Sample Writing Organizer 1

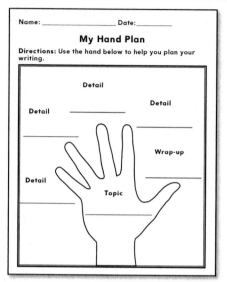

Name: _____ Date:_____

My Hand Plan

Directions: Use the hand below to help you plan your writing.

Detail

Detail _____ Detail

Wrap-up

Detail

Topic

(Gentry, McNeel, and Wallace-Nesler 2012 b–c)

Step 2: Drafting

Drafting—writing it down—is what happens after a student picks up his or her pencil and begins. It's when ideas become words, phrases, sentences, and paragraphs. It is the preliminary version of a text that gets written with the expectation that it will be redrafted. Drafting is generally easier and quicker if students spend time, thought, and effort on prewriting. It should mostly engage the writer in thinking about substance and meaning. With young beginners, drafting may be egocentric, with no notion of an audience in mind. Young writers do not draft in silence. They are often observed talking to themselves, rehearsing, or sounding out words letter by letter. It can be exhilarating if the writer goes back, reads the draft, and thinks, "My goodness, this is great! Did I write that?" Or it can be just the opposite.

It's important for students to recognize that drafting doesn't have to be perfect. Stress that the drafting stage is important for getting thoughts down and finding one's stride or getting in the flow of writing. Since drafting is hard work, teachers often need to cut their students a little slack and not interrupt during this stage. The writer may be deep in thought. If drafters are suffering from "writer's block," they may need encouragement. Sometimes we like to quote the author Joyce Carol Oates to show students how professional authors sometimes feel about drafting. Oates said, "Getting the first draft finished is like pushing a peanut with your nose across a very dirty floor" (Oates 2013). Students seem to get exactly what Oates is talking about.

Graves once remarked that a first draft isn't real writing because real writing goes through a process (as cited in Walshe 1982). In some ways, his notion was like Picasso's idea that a painting isn't real art unless the artist makes a mistake. As with real art, real writing takes on a life of its own. The writer doesn't really know exactly how the product will evolve or what it will look like in the end. Real writing involves both intuition and deliberate action. It's not simply slapping paint on the canvas or throwing down the first words that come to mind and leaving them untouched. Real writing, in Graves's view, starts with revision. He explained it this way: "Writing only truly becomes writing in revision. A professional's first draft is often not much better than anyone else's. It is chiefly in revision that the professional's experience and craftsmanship show" (Walshe 1982, 13). Keep in mind that we sometimes tell our students to push that peanut across the floor with their nose so that they can get to the fun part—revising!

Figure 3.3 Sample Writing Organizer 2

(Gentry, McNeel, and Wallace-Nesler 2012 b–c)

Step 3: Revising

Revising is making content changes to make a piece of writing better. It's not about editing for correctness. Most teachers agree that the two—editing and revision—should be separated because each requires sharpened focus. For beginners, revision is mostly adding on. Later students revise not only by adding on but also by taking out, choosing different words, and reorganizing.

Revision is perhaps the stage where students can learn most as writers. Individual learning is often driven by the teacher's conference. Chapters 2 and 6 explain how to confer with writers. Writing researcher Lucy Calkins says, "A writing conference may be merely a finger-tip on the shoulder or an encouraging word. Or a writing conference may be a fifteen-minute group discussion about a shared problem" (1982, 53). During the writing conference, give responsibility to the writer and listen, observe, question, and extend.

The following are examples of questions to help students focus on content during revision conferences:

- What do you want to say?
- Which part do you like best? Can you make it better?
- What else does your reader need to know?
- Why is this part important?
- Does it sound right when you read it?
- Have you put yourself in this piece?
- Can you change the order around to make it flow better?
- Can you add stronger words or take some words out?
- What do you need to add?
- Are you using vivid verbs?
- Are you using strong adjectives?

Graves playfully thought of revising as "messing up" the first draft. "Young writers need to learn a whole repertoire for messing up their first drafts as they change pieces, insert, take out, reorganize. When students stop erasing and instead cross out, draw lines and arrows, or change handwriting from careful printing to a functional scrawl (knowing this to be only a draft) they show awareness that draft writing is temporary, malleable, meant to be changed" (Walshe 1982, 13). Often, we move students through the writing process and expect them to fully understand the art of revision. It is not an easy method for students to understand and follow through with in their own writing. We must provide a multitude of mini-lessons and examples, along with a lot of encouragement before expecting students to grasp this challenging strategy. Use texts you created or student texts collected from previous years to model the revision process. Provide students time to practice the revision process using drafts they have filed in their folders as finished. The more practice they have with previous drafts, the more likely revisions will become part of their writing process.

Step 4: Editing

If revision is "messing up" the first draft, editing is "fixing it up" for conventions. The focus is correct conventions such as capitalization, grammar usage, punctuation, and spelling. Some students like the notion that we mess up our writing first and then fix it. Targeting specific skills during editing, such as capitalization of proper nouns, reduces a student's feelings of helplessness or becoming overwhelmed when faced with editing for multiple errors. Initially, begin using editing conventions taught and modeled during writer's workshop mini-lessons. Gradually develop your editing checklist to promote successful and confident writers.

We'll consider conventions more in depth in Chapter 6. For now, here's one of our favorite ways to help young writers remember what to look for when editing. We introduce the acronym CUPS, a memorable way for students to remember what to look for when editing: C is for Capitalization, U is for Usage and grammar, P is for Punctuation, and S is for spelling (see Figure 3.4). Use conventions in mini-lessons to focus attention and model each of the CUPS aspects for fixing up papers according to grade appropriate expectations. Then, gradually release responsibility to students as they learn to "CUPS" their papers for editing. Once conventions are taught, turn CUPS into a verb—writers take action! Writing that is student edited then goes into a basket for teacher editing, and students prepare for a final conference before publishing.

Figure 3.4 Sample Conventions Activity

(Gentry, McNeel, and Wallace-Nesler 2012 c–d)

Step 5: Publishing

Publishing makes writing real and gives it purpose. Graves thought that publishing for a real audience was equally important in choice of topic and control of writing by the child (Walshe 1982). Students are inspired by publishing their own writing. They want other students in their writer's workshop to see their published work and often view the classroom audience as being just as important as the teacher. Class books, newsletters, bulletin boards, or magazines can be important starting points. A wider audience may include families and extended families, other classes, the students' school, other schools, members of the community, and even famous or important people. Endless publishing opportunities also exist through social media and the Internet. Commercial websites even make it easy to use templates to publish affordable individual and classroom books that rival the hardback bound quality of the books in the library.

The use of word processing programs provides the means to publish, not just in language arts but also across the curriculum areas, such as letters, brochures, and classroom/school newsletters. Slide–presentation program projects can easily be published into book format, developed into eBooks, or added to the school/class website. Technology allows collaborative projects and sharing among students in other districts, states, and countries. For example, with guardian permission, students may share with new audiences in real time, using technology such as Skype™.

Tips to Enhance the Publishing Process

- Provide a variety of models and examples to support students as they create their own publications.

- Invite an author to share publishing tips, or visit an author's website and ask questions about publishing.

- Provide time, space, and materials that promote and encourage student writing and illustrating and encourage creativity.

- Support students during publishing with parent volunteers or student helpers.

- Provide opportunities to share publications (e.g., bulletin boards, author celebrations, and websites).

Good writing is like a great piece of art not only in how it is crafted but also in how it speaks to others. Good writing captures the essence of something and presents it in a unique way—the crux of an argument that gives the reader an "aha" moment, the essential discovery captured in a scientific report, or the life-changing revelation in a story. Author Rachel Howard (2013) says a writer must move consciousness "out of information-organizing mode into an intuitive way of seeing" (9). The writer, like the artist, sees something differently, and the writer expresses it in print. In Rachel Howard's (2013) words, the author sees it "deeply enough to capture the vibrancy of life on the page" (9). Teaching the process of writing is intended to get students started in that direction. Teaching students in writer's workshop is a joy. Teachers see young writers in writer's workshop capturing the vibrancy of life every day.

Reflect and Review

1. Reflect on your craft. What steps can you take personally and professionally to become more "process" oriented and less "product" oriented as a writing teacher?

2. How do conversation and discussion support prewriting, developing ideas, and planning?

3. What prewriting tools have you found to be most effective with your students? How might you adapt them to include information from this chapter?

4. In what ways might you help students become more fluent during the drafting process?

5. What strategies do you currently use for teaching revision and editing to your students? Share/discuss with your colleagues.

Chapter 4

The Natural Beginnings of Writing, Reading, and Spelling

"Learning to read and learning to spell are one and the same, almost."

—Dr. Linnea Ehri (1997, 237)

Read the following two quotes from two of the many brain-imaging studies that are contributing new understandings of how literacy begins. Results from brain scan studies such as these are unequivocal: reading, writing, and spelling go hand in hand for the development of brain circuitry for literacy.

"Through a series of studies using functional Magnetic Resonance Imaging (fMRI) to probe how the brain processes stimuli in real time, we have demonstrated that, a) there is a distinct system in the human brain that is recruited during reading that is also recruited during writing, b) the reading network develops as a function of handwriting experience, and c) handwriting, and not keyboarding, leads to adult-like neural processing in the visual system of the preschool child. These findings suggest that self-generated action, in the form of handwriting, is a crucial component in setting up brain systems for reading acquisition. There is support for the notion that handwriting instruction is positively connected to learning to read."

—Dr. Karin Harman James (2012, 1)

"Although it is well understood that spelling skills are necessary for successful written communication, spelling and reading may also have a direct reciprocal influence on each other's acquisition."

—Elizabeth S. Norton, Ioulia Kovelman, and
Laura-Ann Petitto (2007, 56)

Beginning reading, writing, and spelling comingle in the brain. You can see evidence of this development if you know what behaviors to look for in very young students' writing because the writing changes qualitatively at each phase. The phases can be used to track any child's progress from the very beginning as he or she progresses through five parallel developmental phases of writing, reading, and spelling to crack the English code in order to convey meaning. This chapter explains why teachers should teach writing and reading alongside each other in preschool, kindergarten, and first grade, with a great deal of emphasis on writing to support literacy acquisition.

In this chapter, we show you the five phases of beginning writing, spelling, and reading. Phase 0, the first phase of writing, should begin in preschool followed by four additional phases that spiral upward generally through the end of first grade. In these five beginning phases, the child moves from no literacy to acquisition of basic brain functioning for both reading and writing. In other words, by the end of first grade, the child's brain should have laid down basic literacy circuitry, at which time the child's reading/writing brain should function much like the proficient reading/writing adult brain functions. By the end of first grade, it's expected that the code is broken, and the child can both encode and decode (write and read) independently, fluently, and with automaticity—at least at the end of first grade levels. The child can read easy chapter books and craft meaningful, interesting pieces of writing following basic conventions. We refer to the five developmental phases as Phase 0, Phase 1, Phase 2, Phase 3, and Phase 4. These phases are five qualitative changes in writing, spelling, and reading that occur in sync in preschool through the end of first grade, if not sooner. Research now shows that during this beginning period of development, writing, reading, and spelling have direct reciprocal influence on one another's acquisition (Berninger 2012; Ehri 1997; Gentry 2010; Graham and Hebert 2012; Norton, Kovelman, and Petitto 2007).

Research that grew out of Piagetian theory has matched early developmental phases of word reading with the same phases of beginning writing and invented spelling. After comparing phases of word reading with early developmental phases of spelling in writing, reading researcher Linnea Ehri described the beginning reading/writing/spelling connection succinctly: "Learning to read and learning to spell are one and the same, almost" (1997, 237). We can see a teacher use the observation of parallel development of reading and writing phases in practice in this snapshot of a teacher's brief writing conference with Mike in a first-grade writer's workshop. Ms. Barnes is, in effect, teaching reading and writing across both curriculums. Sometimes, she has students write to support what they are learning in reading class, at other times, as in the following example, she teaches reading skills in the context of their writing. Observe Ms. Barnes teach Mike as both a writer and a reader as she confers with him in writer's workshop and targets instruction based on his specific needs.

Ms. Barnes' Writing Conference with Mike

The day in Ms. Barnes' classroom begins with a 45-minute writer's workshop before moving into a 90-minute reading block. Each block has specific routines, but Ms. Barnes recognizes how powerfully the writing and reading processes overlap—especially for students who come to her as struggling readers or in early beginning reading phases. As she conducts a brief writer's workshop conference with Mike, who is writing about a picture of his motorboat, she is thinking of his development both as a reader and a writer. Commenting first on meaning, she praises the piece and takes note of his Phase 2 writing—*MY MOTR BT*—which demonstrates partial phonemic awareness with *BT* for boat.

Ms. Barnes: Mike, that's a great start. What does your motorboat do?

Mike: Goes fast.

Ms. Barnes: May I put these two 'magic lines' here so that you can add *goes fast* to your sentence? "My motorboat goes fast!"

She reads as she points to his words reading *goes fast* as she points to her two magic lines. After modeling, she asks Mike to read the whole line as she points to the words. He rereads as she points to his kid writing, and he has a clear understanding of what to do next in his story.

Mike: My motorboat goes fast!

Ms. Barnes: Adding "goes fast" will make your writing much more interesting. You may even want to add some more interesting details about your motorboat.

Ms. Barnes will touch base again to see how Mike is coming along. When he's ready, she may add adult underwriting—a copy of his story in the same line order and word order that he has used—and tape it below his piece to give him a conventional model that he can read back. She considers her conventional copy of his writing (adult underwriting) to be a form of publication and notes that even struggling writers love coming back to reread their piece over and over from the conventional version, which aids their reading fluency. In her words, "reading back adult underwriting is a great reading lesson, and it boosts a beginner's confidence as a writer!"

Ms. Barnes has the option to extend Mike's reading lesson in writer's workshop to include targeted teachable moments for learning about sounds and spelling. She knows that Phase 2 readers and writers typically pay attention to beginning and ending sounds, but Phase 3 readers and writers move into full phonemic awareness paying attention to all the sounds in a word. This is exactly where Mike is functioning as both a reader and a writer. So, she uses the writing conference as the teachable moment to show Mike how to finger-spell each sound in *boat*. Beginning with his thumb, he holds up a finger as he says /b/, then /ŏ/, then /t/ calling attention to the three fingers. Next she draws three sound and letter boxes shown in Figure 4.1, and he finger-spells boat again, this time supplying a letter in the appropriate box after he says each sound.

Figure 4.1 Sample Sound/Letter Box for *Boat*

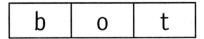

b	o	t

As Ms. Barnes scaffolds, Mike is able to edit for spelling. He moves from BT, a partial phonemic spelling at Phase 2, to BOT, which demonstrates the full phonemic awareness that is Phase 3. Even though Mike reads *boat* correctly from the adult underwriting by repeated readings and memory reading, he's just now learning to focus on all the sounds when he reads or writes words, and he is moving toward full phonemic awareness as he advances from Phase 2 to Phase 3. "In this writing conference, I knew exactly what targeted reading instruction Mike needed to advance as a reader by looking at what he was doing in his writing," Mrs. Barnes explains. "I can see the reading/writing connection as I monitor each child's phase of development. I no longer see reading and writing as entirely separate subjects, but I watch writing, reading, and sound/spelling skills develop in concert as the child moves through five phases of beginning reading, writing, and invented spelling."

Bring Reading Lesson Material into Writer's Workshop, and Vice Versa

Ms. Barnes also effortlessly shifts across the reading and writing blocks by sometimes using content from her reading lessons. For example, a read-aloud text can be used as the model or mentor text to teach a skill, trait, or technique in writer's workshop. "I'm teaching reading and writing all day long," she explains. "Observing my students write shows me how they are thinking about letter-sound correspondence and how they are attending to meaning. It's often in the slowed-down writing process that many of my beginning readers put all the pieces together and learn to read. They are learning to read by writing! But when I introduce a read-aloud book and show them how a real author has used dialogue bubbles to make the characters speak, I'm teaching a writing technique—from a read-aloud book from our reading block. This cross-curricular work is an efficient use of time because we are using some of the same mentor texts for engaging writers that we use to engage them as readers."

There is a rich evidence base demonstrating that writing improves reading (Graham and Hebert 2012) and a solid evidence base for phase observation (Ehri 1997, 2000; Gentry 2006, 2010). Figure 4.2 shows what reading strategies the student is using alongside writing strategies and letter-sound strategies in each of the five phases. These charts will help you know what to expect in each phase and help you target instruction specific to the student's needs.

How to Use the Five Phases of Beginning Writing, Spelling, and Reading Charts

The charts for each phase, (Figure 4.2 and Appendix C) show what strategies a student is using for writing, reading, and sounds/spelling in each developmental phase. That is to say, each chart shows which strategies go hand-in-hand in a particular phase. Match each beginning reader and writer in your class to one of the phase charts. Use these cross-curricular charts to help you show parents where a student is at the beginning of the year and how the student is progressing developmentally as a reader and writer throughout the year. Remember that these charts may span development from preschool to end of first grade.

Figure 4.2 Five Phases of Beginning Spelling, Reading, and Writing

Phase 0	Spelling/ Sound Awareness Looks Like:	Word Reading Looks Like:	Guided Reading Looks Like:	Writing Looks Like:	Writing Sample
Preschool or sooner	No Spelling May clap syllables May shout out rhyming words	Reads memorized sight words or phrases May pretend to read	Responds to read-alouds with repeated reading and dialogue reading Memory reading of words and phrases and favorite books	Characterized by marking, drawing, and scribbling, leading to letter-like forms	

Phase 1	Spelling/ Sound Awareness Looks Like:	Word Reading Looks Like:	Guided Reading Looks Like:	Writing Looks Like:	Writing Sample
First half of kinder. sooner	Writes letters but no attention to sounds Claps syllables Shouts out rhyming words No phonemic awareness in evidence	Reads envrionmental print Has little capacity to "sound out" Relies on pictures, logographic memory, or guessing Ehri's Pre-alphabetic Phase: Child sees *Crest®* and says *toothpaste*; sees the *golden arches* and says *McDonald's®*	Memory reading of Level A easy books	Attempts to write messages and stories using letters	 **A flock of butterflies**

Phase 2	Spelling/ Sound Awareness Looks Like:	Word Reading Looks Like:	Guided Reading Looks Like:	Writing Looks Like:	Writing Sample
End of kinder. or sooner	Writes using beginning and ending letter-sound correspondences	Reads memorized sight words Cues words using beginning, ending, or prominent letters Ehri's Partial-alphabetic Phase: sees *ink* and says *ice*; sees *klug* and says *king*.	Memory reading of Level A–C easy books	Labels drawings or writes message with a few letter-sound matches	HMT DPD **Humpty Dumpty**

Phase 3	Spelling/ Sound Awareness Looks Like:	Word Reading Looks Like:	Guided Reading Looks Like:	Writing Looks Like:	Writing Sample
First half of first grade or sooner	Spells with a letter for each sound Has full phonemic awareness; e.g., *night* spelled NIT for /n/+/i/+/t/; *came* spelled CAM for /k/+/ā/+/m/	Reads many more known sight words Ehri's Full-alphabetic Phase: Distinguishes similarly spelled words such as *king* and *kick*; uses knowledge of *pink* to figure out *ink*	Memory reading of Level C–G easy books	Writes by attending to one letter for each sound Employs growing conventionally-spelled word recognition vocabulary	tuth FaRe wn nit I ws n mi BeD and the tuth FaRe cam.

Phase 4	Spelling/ Sound Awareness Looks Like:	Word Reading Looks Like:	Guided Reading Looks Like:	Writing Looks Like:	Writing Sample
End of first grade or sooner	Spells many words correctly Operates with a chunking strategy when inventing unknown words (e.g., chunks phonics patterns) *buildings* spelled BILLDINGS; *everywhere* spelled EVREWHAIR	Reads over 100 words automatically Cues on chunks Accurately decodes nonsense words: *yode, fler, cleef* Recognizes syllable units in polysyllabic words: *man* in hu*man*; com*mand*	Reads more independently without gradual release model Independent reading of Level G–I easy chapter books	Writes showing an awareness of phonics patterns Writes using conventional spelling patterns	My feet getishb. I whair sis 3. My feet take me evrewhair. My feet like to clime trees and billdings I walk to school. My feet make me swem in water. My feet are tiyerd at the end of the day. **My foot**

(Adapted from Raising Confident Readers: How to Teach Your Child to Read and Write—From Baby to Age 7, Gentry 2010)

Tips for Matching Students to a Phase

Take several samples of a student's writing and list all the invented spellings:

➤ If the student is using scribbles and letter-like forms but no letters, the student is in Phase 0.

➤ If most of the invented spellings use letters but the letters do not correspond to sounds in the word, the student is in Phase 1.

➤ If most of the invented spellings demonstrate letter-sound correspondence for beginning, ending, or prominent sounds, the student is exhibiting partial phonemic awareness and is in Phase 2.

➤ If most of the invented spellings demonstrate letter-sound correspondence representing all of the sounds in the word, the student is exhibiting full phonemic awareness and is in Phase 3.

➤ If most of the invented spellings are in chunks of acceptable spelling patterns that fit the sounds or syllables in the word, and if CVC short vowel patterns are generally spelled correctly, the student is in Phase 4.

As students continue to develop through the phases and beyond, good writers are likely students who enjoy reading, who read voraciously (and closely), and who use reading and favorite authors as models for their writing. While it's not uncommon to find students who read well but who have not developed into writers, it's rare to find a good writer who is not a good reader.

In the next chapter, we look at writing across the curriculum in disciplinary areas. If we are to have students who write well in disciplinary areas, they must read deeply in these areas and use their reading to shape their writing. Not only must they read deeply, they must read the literature specific to the discipline. Each discipline—science, math, literature, geography, engineering, history—has its own distinctive structure, format, and language conventions for writing. One of the goals of writing across the curriculum is to introduce students to modes of writing specific to the disciplines.

Reflect and Review

1. If you are working with a student at the beginning stages of writing, use the charts in Figure 4.2 to match each of your students to one of the five phases of reading, writing, and spelling development and monitor his/her progress through the phases. Match each of your students to a phase by looking at the student's writing, invented spelling, and guided reading level.

2. Once you match each student to one of the five phases, determine how you might use this information when planning for instruction during whole-group, small-group, and individualized instruction.

3. Can you use these cross-curricular charts in parent conferences to show a child's literacy development from lower to higher phases? Show parents where their child is on the five-phase continuum from no writing in Phase 0 to proficient reading and writing expected in Phase 4.

Chapter 5

Close Reading, Inquiry-Based Learning, and Writing Across the Curriculum

"Reader and writer, we wish each other well. Don't we want and don't we understand the same thing?"

—Eudora Welty (1994, xxvi)

Eudora Welty's quote encapsulates exactly what Writing Across the Curriculum does for students in subject-area study and why we want students who are studying science, math, social studies, history, and the like to not only read about these subjects but also to engage in them with inquiry-based learning and also as writers. Writing enables students to learn more and requires them to think more deeply in the subject area. In Chapter 5, we demonstrate how writing inspires students to read more closely in subject areas, do inquiry projects, and develop understanding. Writing about any topic helps to clarify thinking and opens the gate for more learning. As Welty points out, if one wants to *understand* something, not only should one read about it, but one should write about it as well. Close reading, inquiry, and writing all work together to help boost understanding. Our experience as authors has taught us that writing clarifies our thinking and understanding and that of our students. You will see this happening with your students, too.

Writing Across the Curriculum not only values writing as a method of learning but also recognizes differences in writing conventions across disciplines. Historians, scientists, mathematicians, and newspaper editors write differently in different forms for different audiences. Writing Across the Curriculum is a pedagogical approach, popularized in the 1980s.

It promoted the idea that students should engage in discipline-specific writing conventions at all grade levels. A kindergarten student can make an observation and write like a scientist just as the fourth-grade student or the eighth-grade student can write like a scientist, but at different levels of sophistication.

Writing Across the Curriculum is a highly regarded instructional practice in most curriculums across the country. More than ever, teachers in all disciplines are being asked to use writing as an instructional tool in their teaching. With writing being identified as a top skill that employers look for when hiring new employees (Hart Research Associates 2010), students must be provided with multiple opportunities to write in a variety of disciplines. Not only do students reap the benefits of practicing discipline-specific writing conventions, but also Writing Across the Curriculum enhances student achievement.

We begin by exploring close reading and inquiry-based learning. Then we *show* how writing across the curriculum can use close reading, inquiry, and writing together. Next, we dive more deeply into Writing Across the Curriculum and explore its two main parts: Writing to Learn in the disciplines and Learning to Write in the disciplines, the latter as in learning to write like a scientist, like a historian, or like the writers in whatever discipline is being studied in the elementary school curriculum.

Close Reading

The connection between writing and close reading is straightforward: writing and close reading are reciprocal. Richard Paul and Linda Elder (2014) state that "both require that we think from multiple perspectives; both require that we use the elements of reasoning well" (3). Doing one helps students do the other. That is to say, students will read closely to become better writers in content-area study and in doing so, they also become better readers of the content of the discipline. Before we go further, however, let's first define "close reading," which many teachers find confusing.

Close reading is often compared to digging a hole. Each time we put in the shovel and remove the dirt, we move deeper into the ground. In the same way, close reading is reading and rereading text to "dig deeper" into the meaning. We want to go further with that analogy and suggest close reading is also the seed you plant in that hole that leads to independent, thoughtful readers. As teachers, we want our students to be excited, connected, and engaged in the reading process as well as develop a passion for reading. Close reading opens our students' eyes, hearts, and minds by noticing, questioning, and wondering not just about the text but also how that text relates to their lives and the world around them. Kylene Beers and Robert Probst (2013) see close reading as a method to bring the text and reader *close* together.

> "Close reading should suggest close attention to the text; close attention to the relevant experience, thought, and memory of the reader; close attention to the responses and interpretations of other readers; and close attention to the interactions among those elements."
>
> —Beers and Probst (2013, 36)

Chris Lehman and Kate Roberts (2013) share a simple structure to help students develop independent habits during close reading: read through lenses, use lenses to find patterns, and use the patterns to develop a new understanding of the text. When entering the first step, reading through lenses, we determine what we will focus our attention on in the text (e.g., organizational structure, word choice, and character traits, as well as gathering information relevant to our focus). As we analyze that information, we search for relationships and patterns and determine commonalities and/or contradictions. Finally, we use our newfound knowledge to develop our personal interpretation of the text before us.

In his blog "Shanahan on Literacy," reading researcher Tim Shanahan gives a simple but succinct definition of close reading. He says that close reading, sometimes called "critical reading," "analytical reading," or "deep reading," requires the reader to go beyond what one might glean from one reading alone. Close reading simply involves multiple readings or partial targeted re-readings, allowing the reader to dig deeper into the text. A second or third close reading might allow the reader to figure out not only what the text means but also how it works. Close reading allows for more contemplation, analysis, synthesis, reflection, and evaluation than the first reading alone. Close reading is necessary in subject-area study in order for students to understand the content being studied and to plan for writing responses such as summaries, retellings, and comparisons.

According to Shanahan, close reading might answer the following questions:

- How did the author organize the text?
- What literary devices were used, and how effective were they?
- What was the quality of the presentation?
- If used, how was data or evidence presented?
- Why did the author choose particular words?
- Was the author consistent in his/her presentation?

(Shanahan 2012)

Other close reading questions might lead the reader to think about deeper meaning, such as "Why is this piece important for me to dig into?"; "What is the author's stance or voice?"; "How does this impact what I already know?"; "How does this text connect to other texts that I have read?"; "What makes this piece aesthetically pleasing?" Close reading may also be strategic in finding specific information that one needs, such as the main idea of a paragraph. Close reading connects to writing because questions such as these are many of the same ones that student writers must contemplate in developing a good piece of writing. Both readers and writers develop an understanding of how close reading can support the writer's development of purpose, audience, organizational structure, word choice, sentence fluency, and presentation.

To help understand the relationship of close reading to writing, let's "look through the lens" and consider one of the quality traits of good writing: word choice. Christopher Lehman and Kate Roberts (2013) view word choice as a fundamental close reading skill, stating, "Looking closely at word choice allows us to get to the heart of what people are saying and thinking; it helps us to see their motivation more clearly and decide how we wish to understand them" (33). It is with this same understanding that a writer carefully selects specific words to create the "voice," or tone, of the writing, which in turn affects the meaning for the reader.

In *Hello Ocean* (2003), the story of a young girl's visit to the ocean, author Pam Muñoz Ryan creates the tone of her message through deliberate word and phrase choices.

Amber seaweed,

speckled sand,

bubbly waves

that kiss the land,

I touch the ocean,

and the surf gives chase,

then wraps me in a wet embrace.

(5 and 14)

Through close reading of just these excerpts, we use lenses to find patterns and explore how words are used to set the tone of the text. Ryan's word choice of *bubbly* and *chase* both imply playfulness, while *kiss* and *embrace* invoke feelings of love. Looking back at Lehman and Roberts (2013), we use the patterns to develop a new understanding of the text. It is safe to say the author is "thinking" of the ocean as a place to have fun and a place she dearly loves to visit. Although a simple example, by using this information, we can support young writers as they begin to understand the use of denotation and connotation of words to influence and affect their readers' reactions and emotions to their text (see Figure 5.1).

Figure 5.1 Sample Word Connotation

The Power of Connotation

Authors select specific words that may influence and affect their readers' reactions and emotions.

Denotation is a word's dictionary definition.

Snake: one of many scaly reptile species

The _snake_ slithered through the tall grass.

Connotation is the emotional feelings, images, and memories that accompany a word. It is what comes to mind when you read or hear the word.

Snake: evil, danger, dishonest, treachery, creepy

The salesman was like a _snake_ ready to strike.

Compare each pair of sentences below that have the same denotative meaning but different connotations.

That girl is smart.	The watch is inexpensive.
That girl is brainy.	The watch is cheap.

Your Turn:

For each of these words, write synonyms with positive and negative connotations. For example:

Denotation	Positive Connotation	Negative Connotation
heavy	plump	fat or obese

- short
- stubborn

- child
- politician

- smart
- nice

(Gentry, McNeel, and Wallace-Nesler 2013 g)

To support your students' understanding of close reading, it is important to scaffold their learning and build toward independence. Following are a few close reading tools teachers find helpful in their instruction. We encourage you to explore the close reading strategies of Lehman and Roberts (2013), Beers and Probst (2013) , and Shanahan (2012).

First, develop an anchor chart with students to support their understanding of close reading. This is one example of a classroom chart:

Close Reading is...

Carefully reading and rereading the text

Looking for big ideas and key details

Observing and noting organization, word choice, and patterns

Searching for evidence

Explaining the evidence. How? Why?

During the reading and rereading, encourage students to annotate the text, using symbols and sticky notes to identify noteworthy text elements that help clarify meaning. This process allows students to slow down their thinking and notice key ideas and details and how the author uses craft and text structure. Ultimately, students use the annotations to share and support their thinking through discussions or through some form of writing. Each of these symbols is specifically modeled and practiced with students and accumulated into a list for students to use independently. The symbols in Figure 5.2 are a few examples of those used for annotating text.

Figure 5.2 Sample of Text Symbols for Close Reading

Symbol	Text Symbol Cue	Explanation of Text Symbol
★	This is important to the main idea or supports the main idea.	A star identifies the main idea of the text, along with any other important details that support and clarify the main idea.
✓	I agree … This verifies my prediction.	The checkmark notes when the student agrees with the author's point of view or verifies a prediction made before or during reading.
?	I have a question about … Why did the author … I wonder …	A question mark in the text is used when the student has questions or the text piques their curiosity in some way.
___	I do not understand this word.	Underlining is used to mark unfamiliar words and vocabulary to revisit and look up later.
O	I want to remember this word, phrase, or pattern!	Interesting words, phrases, and/or patterns that may clarify text meaning are circled.
TS	This helps me identify the text structure the author used.	*TS* might include diagrams, graphs, transition words, or other features that identify the text structures: description, sequence and order, compare and contrast, cause and effect, problem and solution.

Symbol	Text Symbol Cue	Explanation of Text Symbol
C	That reminds me of a time when … This is different from … (or the same as …) I read another book/article …	*C* is used when making connections to ideas, experiences, etc. in the text that may be text to self, text to text, or text to world.
!	Now I see why … OK, so the author's point is … I learned that …	Exclamation marks the "aha" moments that happen during reading the text that the student discovers all on his or her own without the author coming out and saying it.

Helping young writers bridge an awareness of how they can use close reading to explore author's purpose, text structures, literary devices, word choice, voice, and presentation opens the dialogue to Writing Across the Curriculum and will empower them to use these strategies in their writing.

Inquiry-Based Learning

Classrooms using inquiry-based learning may appear to be unorganized and quite simply "playing." On the contrary, these classrooms have boundaries and organizational structures that support, monitor, and challenge students to be creative, inquisitive risk takers. These classrooms are full of wonder, places where students are not just "doing projects" but are engaged in learning that emerges from an innate curiosity that naturally fosters interaction—communicating, questioning, connecting, inferring, problem-solving, and reflecting. Learning is enhanced when the quality and quantity of student involvement is increased and teachers facilitate, model, coach, and guide students through the inquiry process.

Inquiry-based learning is best defined by Kuklthau, Maniotes and Caspari. "Inquiry is an approach to learning whereby students find and use a variety of sources of information and ideas to increase their understanding of a problem, topic, or issue of importance. It requires more than simply answering questions or getting a right answer. It espouses investigation, exploration, search, quest, research, pursuit, and study. It is enhanced by involvement with a community of learners, each learning from the other in social interaction." (2007, 2)

It is through inquiry and the sense of wonderment that writers may discover their next big idea for writing, a story lead, or even a poetry title. Ralph Fletcher refers to it as a writer's "fierce wonderings." Those memories, images, and words that linger on our minds during reading are the same ones that make writers start asking "big, open-ended questions that have no easy answers" (1996, 18). These can often lead to a student's best writing. Allowing students to be inquisitive and to discover and make decisions about their learning, creates a sense of ownership, pride, and self-motivation.

When we teach through inquiry, we are guiding students through a process—a dynamic process that has taken on a number of different but similar models. No matter what the specific inquiry process steps, the outcome is an authentic learning experience created through our students' genuine curiosity; their "fierce wonderings."

Based on The Newport News Public Schools Inquiry Process, Sabrina Carnesi and Karen DiGiorgio (2009, 32–36) identify six steps with specific tasks that are part of an interactive cycle of the inquiry process. Students continuously reflect, revise, and evaluate before moving on to the next step. Their process includes:

- **Questioning:** Students generate a meaningful list of questions inspired by curiosity and include open-ended questions of *who*, *what*, *where*, *when*, *why*, and *how*. What makes the moon change shape? Where does the moon go? What happened to the sun? Questions sometimes emerge during inquiry and redefine the direction of the inquiry.

- **Planning:** During this step, students create a plan to complete their projects on time. This will also allow an opportunity to ensure that they have a clear understanding of the expectations of the project. Students might review previous student projects and explore resources best suited for their inquiry project.

- **Collecting and Crediting:** At this point, students begin collecting and sorting information to determine which is most relevant to the inquiry questions. It is important that students are careful to record source information to be used when citing the reference. Provide support to the class, small group, or individuals with citing sources based on the needs of students. Collecting can take on different forms, like the crafting of an experiment, observing and recording procedures and outcomes, and interviewing experts.

- **Organizing:** Students plan and organize their findings into a format that represents their final product. They may wish to use a graphic organizer to determine if they need additional information. For example, completing a persuasive map graphic organizer may show the lack of examples to support the opinion of the writer.

- **Synthesizing:** Once students organize their resources, they become insightful about new thoughts and knowledge and begin to draw conclusions. Students complete their final products, selecting from a variety of format options (e.g., multimedia presentation, report, brochure, blog, digital portfolio page, speech, and page of a classroom book).

- **Communicating:** Unlike the end of traditional projects in which students simply hand in their projects to await the teacher's final reward, the inquiry process encourages sharing, publishing, and celebrating the students' accomplishment. Through communication of their newfound knowledge, students have the opportunity to teach others and become a part of a classroom community of investigators, readers, and writers whose thoughts and ideas are expected and accepted.

Throughout this inquiry process, students reflect, revise, and evaluate each step before moving onto the next. The process encourages collaboration and communication building in an environment where students are comfortable asking questions and reflecting on the outcome.

In summary, engaging students in inquiry-based learning allows them to build knowledge by conducting investigations of a topic, problem, or issue; gathering information; analyzing or synthesizing the information; and creating solutions or new understanding. Actively involve students through inquiry in content-area study rather than passively sitting back, taking notes from a lecture, memorizing facts, and regurgitating them on a test. Teaching through inquiry exemplifies the familiar adage, *Tell me, I'll forget. Show me, I may remember. But involve me, and I'll understand.* Student writers often begin the inquiry by creating questions to be researched, writing down or collecting evidence, followed by explanations and synthesis, solutions, arguments, or justifications scripted in notes or some other format. The entire inquiry process involves a variety of forms of written communication. Writing, then, is one of the fundamental tools of inquiry.

Using Writing, Close Reading, and Inquiry Together Close reading, writing through inquiry, use of multiple texts, and use of technology are often combined in a unit of disciplinary study. The following is one of our favorite examples from Justin Minkel (2013), an award winning second-and third-grade teacher from Arkansas. He shows us how to engage students in close reading and inquiry on a primary topic by using multiple sources and having students write about it. In the unit that follows, Minkel demonstrates close reading and writing as a result of inquiry in a wonderful second-grade animal study that engages students in deep levels of thinking and creativity. He shows how teachers are responding to the following Common Core Standards (2010) statement: "In K–5, the Standards follow the National Assessment of Educational Progress's lead in balancing the reading of literature with the reading of informational texts, including texts in history/social studies, science, and technical subjects."

Justin Minkel's Science Unit on Animals

Students understand what they create. With the Common Core State Standards shift toward informational text, it isn't enough for students to read more nonfiction. They need to write research papers, manuals, advertisements, and other "out of the box" kinds of writing, too.

Most of us get the reciprocal relationship between reading and writing. With fiction, we ask students to read engaging dialogue, compelling sequences of events, or descriptive sensory writing that makes them feel they're experiencing what the characters experience. The purpose isn't just the pleasure of reading, but to help young writers master the craft of writing great dialogue, plotting out events in a story of their own making, or describing the setting, characters, or objects in a story so clearly the reader can visualize every detail. The same reading-writing connection is true with informational text. When students create their own maps, charts, diagrams, indexes, and glossaries, they understand these features better when they encounter them in a book.

My 2nd graders complete their first research project around the middle of the year, on an animal of their choosing. Pairs who picked the same animal work together to generate questions, using the "I wonder..." stem they do when we read fiction:

"I wonder why rhinos have that big horn for a nose."

"I wonder what an octopus eats."

"I wonder if tigers ever get in fights with other predators."

Once I've pulled together a range of websites along with books from the classroom, school, and public libraries, the research begins. Students take notes on sticky notes about anything that either relates to one of their guiding *"I wonders"* or just seems interesting, surprising, or important to them. Reading this way is fundamentally different for students who have grown up with narratives—bedtime stories, fairy tales, children's movies, picture books—to this point. You'd never turn to the middle page of a fairy tale or chapter book and start reading from there, so students' first impulse with any book is to begin on the page 1 and read on.

When we start reading informational text, I ask my 2nd graders, "If you wanted to use a cookbook to find a recipe for pumpkin pie, would you read the whole cookbook or just turn to the page with that recipe on it?" They laugh, but the idea of being more strategic about finding the information they need is strange to them at first.

We do mini-lessons focus on features like an index, headings, or the table of contents, and they get used to searching for a single page or section that relates to their *"I wonder"* questions (what polar bears eat, the countries where jaguars live) rather than reading the books start-to-finish the way they would read fiction. I learn a lot from the notes they take, like the fact that my students—most of them English learners—tend to over-rely on visual cues. We have had plenty of conversations about misconceptions that arise when they infer meaning from a photograph (e.g., "Wolves cry blood," or my favorite, "Polar bears mate by kissing with their noses") without confirming that fact in the caption or text.

Once the pairs have amassed 20 or 30 notes, we get out huge swaths of butcher paper and organize their sticky notes by clusters of subtopics. Notes that read, Bears are omnivores, Bears eat fish, berries, and honey, and Bear cubs drink milk from their mothers might go together under the topic Bear Food. It's confusing, but liberating, for the 2nd graders to realize there's no single right answer for how to organize their notes. A student will often ask me, "Does this note about bear cubs drinking their mother's milk go in 'Bear Food,' 'Bears Are Mammals,' or 'Bears' Life Cycle?'" The realization that a single fact could fit in multiple sections teaches them something important about organizing complex information. It also makes them think a lot more at lot harder than they do when deciding which answer choice to bubble in on a test or worksheet.

The subtopics students come up with become the headings in their written paper. For each section, like "Bears Are Mammals," students figure out a topic sentence and then figure out how to sequence the notes they've taken. Once the text is done, they create a diagram to go with it, like an "X-Ray Diagram" that shows several piglets curled up in their mother's womb, or a multi-box diagram that shows a sequence of events like a cheetah sneaking up on a gazelle in the first box, chasing the gazelle in the second, and bringing it down in the third. When their report is complete, students go through and underline key words to include in their index or define in their glossary.

Along with the final research paper, students condense their information into a slide show and find images to support the facts on each slide, like a photograph of a piranha skeleton for the note that Piranhas are vertebrates, or a map and key for the countries where piranhas are found. Not surprisingly, the most popular choices of animals to research tend to be the most violent—sharks, tigers, komodo dragons, and pretty much any other animal that bloodily devours its prey. Students present what they learned to the class, with their slides now projected on the interactive whiteboard, while the other students take notes on categories like habitat, classification, and food chain.

The project fits dozens of bulleted science standards into one Understanding by Design guiding question How do animals' bodies help them survive in their habitats? Because of the element of choice and the brainstorming of questions students really want to answer, they tend to plunge into some pretty complex texts with a great deal of persistence and enthusiasm.

The three-week project fits into the our daily structure for writer's workshop: a brief mini-lesson with anchor texts (most drawn from Ralph Fletcher's Nonfiction Craft Lessons K–8), followed by about half an hour *to apply that mini-lesson to reading and writing alone or in pairs, with a few minutes to share and reflect at the end.*

Students learn a lot about reading informational text—how to use an index and glossary, how diagrams work with text to support meaning, and how to read with a purpose when you're seeking the answer to a question, but they also learn to write informational text. They have created their own index and glossary, written headings for the facts they've organized, and thought about what kind of diagram would best support each section. They now have a first-hand understanding of these features of informational text they could never have learned just by reading it.

I have always loved the line, "A child is a candle to be lit, not a cup to be filled." With the shift toward a balance of narrative and informational text, we have to remember these simple truths of teaching. Reading and writing are connected. Our students need to be expressive (speaking and writing) not just receptive (reading and listening). And the most important one "Students understand what they create. If they write it, they'll be able to read it. They'll get a lot smarter along the way, too."

We know of no better example of writing across the curriculum than this masterful example from Justin Minkel. Writing Across the Curriculum in classrooms such as Justin's is authentic and engages students in "Learning to Write" but also in "Writing to Learn."

Writing to Learn and Learning to Write

Writing is a tool for discovery, for understanding, for shaping meaning, and for developing thinking. Writing should be an everyday activity in all classrooms—especially in disciplinary areas—because it's one of the best ways to learn. Writing has become essential for full participation in the workforce. By writing, students of all ages develop their thinking skills. Rather than being consumers of information regurgitating facts, writers in disciplinary areas engage in deeper levels of thinking. Writing Across the Curriculum can have two goals that are not mutually exclusive: Writing to Learn and Learning to Write. Let's explore both goals.

Writing to Learn in the Disciplines

Writing to Learn activities are easy to engage in because they can include frequent, brief, informal writing tasks that engage the student in thinking, applying, and/or reflecting about the main ideas presented during the class. The focus of the writing, when engaging in Writing to Learn activities, is on the student's thinking and understanding of the content, not necessarily on the mechanical skills. Many Writing to Learn pieces don't have to be revised, edited, or made perfect, but students can eventually evolve to produce more formal writing. When students write about their learning, they are also verifying their understanding as well as developing a deeper understanding of the subject matter. In "How Writing Shapes Thinking," Langer and Applebee (1987) explain how adding writing tasks improves comprehension and understanding of content, better than does just reading that content.

Keep in mind that students may not appear in your classroom with the writing skills necessary to succeed in your content area. You are responsible for modeling, scaffolding, and guiding students through the process. Writing in your classroom will not only enhance student achievement in your subject area but will also improve the writing skills of your students in other settings.

Writing to Learn activities can include a variety of writing assignments in different formats and for different audiences including, but not limited to, journals, exit tickets, graphic organizers, observation/learning logs, diagrams, and lists, and eventually move to more sophisticated pieces. As we take you through casual, semiformal, and more formal examples of specific disciplinary writing, keep in mind that all of these examples may be considered Writing to Learn because they are increasing students' learning and understanding.

Learning to Write in the Disciplines

Writing in specific subject areas helps students understand the thinking and writing of a particular discipline and complies with language, conventions, format, and structure typical of that discipline. A poet thinks and writes differently from a scientist or a biographer. Each discipline has its unique language, writing formats, and structures along with discipline-specific conventions and traditions. Ergo, good writing in one discipline does not guarantee that same level of writing in another area. A student may be quite proficient at developing an expressive piece for creative writing but may have difficulty being brief and concise in a science lab report. Writing in the disciplines in elementary and middle school offers a plethora of opportunities for students to explore alternate discipline-specific formats in authentic contexts.

Review the list below. Which formats offer possibilities for the disciplines you teach? Can you provide great examples of writing in the content areas you teach that are personal favorites? Which formats will students enjoy exploring?

• Article	• Alphabet Book	• Autobiography	• Biography	• Blog
• Booklet	• Brochure	• Case Study	• Diary	• Editorial
• Fairy Tale	• Journal	• Interview	• Letter	• Magazine Article
• Manual	• Myth	• Newspaper Article	• Novel	• Play
• Poem	• Popular Article	• Position Paper	• Problem/ Solution	• Report
• Research Paper	• Short Story	• Synthesis Paper	• Textbook Chapter	

Learning to write in discipline-specific formats affords the following advantages:

- Introduces students to discipline-specific thinking and writing models.

- Helps students communicate in the tools of the discipline.

- Promotes deeper thinking and active engagement.

- Provides authentic writing tasks in which students write like scientists, historians, poets, and mathematicians.

- Supports the learning of key concepts, vocabulary, and content.

- Provides one alternative for assessment of student learning.

Tips for Teaching Discipline-Specific Writing

It's helpful to provide students with time for reading and writing by organizing teaching around preplanned topics of study in a yearlong calendar. Provide a clear model of expectations for each formal writing project, and give students a flexible time line and sequence of writing expectations and tasks to help them plan. Follow these five tips to help students meet expectations with confidence:

➤ Inform students in advance of specific expectations.

➤ Follow through with supporting comments by spotlighting how well they meet expectations.

➤ Consider developing a commenting guide or checklist to help comment quickly but thoroughly on the points you decide are most important for the assignment.

➤ Set up a sequence chart with flexible time expectations, building toward the final project.

➤ Make sure the expected tasks build on each other.

To elevate student achievement, develop a Writing Across the Curriculum program in your school in which teachers have a clear understanding of the writing process, the quality traits of writing, and the benefits of teaching writing and reading in their discipline. Encourage communication and collaboration among staff to share ideas and discuss both positive and negative issues of the program. Most importantly, be a writer in your own classroom. If students are writing in their science log to explain the process of photosynthesis, for example, write your own explanation in a science log and share it with the class. If you value writing as a tool for learning, students will become aware of the importance of writing in the classroom.

In his popular online article, "Writing Across the Curriculum," (2013) Steve Peha posts three easy-to-follow guidelines to help disciplinary teachers ease students into writing:

1. Start with some easy casual writing activities on a daily, or every-other-day, basis.

2. Gradually work to two or three more elaborate pieces per month.

3. Engage students in a large formal writing project over six to eight weeks.

There are three categories for easing students into disciplinary writing: casual writing, semiformal writing, and formal writing. Notice his use of the social dress code—casual, semiformal, and formal—as a metaphor for writing in content areas. In essence, these activities go from low stakes, to medium, to high stakes for accomplishment. By easing students into writing in the content-area classroom, they begin writing with confidence, developing routines and choices for disciplinary writing, and avoiding feelings of anxiety that make them dread disciplinary writing as a chore.

Casual Writing: A Come-As-You-Are Thinking Tool

"We use this kind of writing to organize our thoughts, to help us remember, and sometimes just to relax and get our minds working on a problem. I like to think of it as sketching with words. It's rough work, done quickly, that helps us remember, organize, and manage the information of our day-to-day activities."

—Peha (2013, 10)

Formats for Casual Writing

- Notes from readings

- Notes from lessons and lectures

- Lists

- Notes from small-group discussions

- Brainstorms

- Brief descriptions of thought processes and problem-solving approaches

- Free writes

- Maps, webs, and first attempts at organization

- Questions

- Journal responses

- Log responses

(Peha 2013, 10)

Sample Activities for Casual Writing

The following are some sample activities for casual writing.

What I think . . . Why I think it (Peha 2013): Have students write down how they think. Ask them to briefly describe their thought processes in step-by-step procedures for activities such as solving a math problem (e.g., adding two fractions, multiplying a number by $\frac{1}{2}$), completing a lab observation of a dissection, or recording observations of any step-by-step process such as daily observations of eggs hatching in an incubator or daily monitoring of local weather. Have students write down what they think and why they think it.

I think _____ because _____ (list the points)_____ (Point 1, point 2, point 3, etc.).

Believing and Doubting Game (Elbow 1998): Eminent writing researcher Peter Elbow invented the "Believing and Doubting Game" that may begin as a casual writing activity and expand into semiformal or formal writing. First, have writers jot down why they support something. Then have them take the exact opposite position and jot down reasons they can imagine being in opposition to it. This is a great activity for opinion or argumentative pieces for any content area. It can start in kindergarten with opinion pieces such as *Which are better, cats or dogs? Which is better, pie or cake?* It can also be used at any level of academia exploring scientific theory, such as opinions about global warming, in politics, or regarding social issues. The activity always opens the door to more reading and further inquiry.

Semiformal Writing: Conventional yet Comfortable

"Somewhere between the pick-up-your-pencil-and-go quality of casual writing and the thoughtful deliberation of publisher-perfect prose, there lies a vast expanse of pen and paper possibilities. A lot of the writing you'll do in class falls into the semiformal category"

—Peha (2013, 18).

Formats for Semiformal Writing

- Summaries
- Reaction Papers
- Responses
- Drafts
- Reflections
- Informal informational letters, notes, or emails

(Peha 2013, 18)

Sample Activities for Semiformal Writing

Reading/Dialogue Journals: Dialogue journals are letters written back and forth between teacher and student or between peers. They may be kept in a bound journal or marble composition book. Often used for literature studies, they are a useful way for students to reflect on their reading and go deeper in their thinking than simply talking about their book in a peer or teacher conference. Dialogue journals encourage close reading. Consider the following tips for reading/dialogue journals from Nancie Atwell (1998).

Tips for Reading/Dialogue Journals

➤ Consider including correspondence with friends.

➤ Address each letter and put in the date.

➤ Write a half page or more.

➤ Respond to a friend within 24 hours.

➤ Write about how you feel about what you are reading and why.

➤ Ask questions such as:

  ➤ What questions do you have while you are reading?

  ➤ How did the author write?

  ➤ How does this connect with something else you have read?

  ➤ How did you approach reading this book?

  ➤ What did you like or not like, or what are you wondering about?

Formal Writing:
All Dressed Up, Some Place to Go

When describing formal writing, Steve Peha (2013) recounts his own frustrations writing across the curriculum when teachers assigned written reports and graded them often with vapid remarks such as *Good work. B+* or *Please write more legibly.* B-. Peha believes that content-area teachers are now more likely to have students engage in authentic formal writing projects for an audience other than the teacher to show them models of good writing and to help them fix what needs fixing.

> "Most people, when they really think about it, admit that the traditional school report experience just made them dislike serious scholarship and dread formal writing. But all of that is changing, and it is definitely a change for the better."
>
> —Peha (2013, 24)

Formats for Formal Writing

- Research reports
- Business letters and other formal correspondence
- Job applications
- Newspapers or other publications
- Submissions to a school anthology
- Essays for contests
- Published interviews

(Peha 2013, 24)

Sample Activities for Formal Writing

Peha (2013) recommends individualizing formal writing projects and giving students options in choosing a role, a format, an audience, a purpose, and finally an approach for designing a successful formal writing project for the content area. In Figure 5.3, he demonstrates how to set up the assignment. The strategies to be learned—selecting a role, format, audience, purpose, and approach—are really strategies for developing the content, placing meaning at the core of the process.

Figure 5.3 Creating Formal Writing Assignments in the Content Areas

Role	Format	Audience	Purpose	Approach
Choose one or possibly two. Most assignments will have one.	Choose one only. Only in rare cases would combining formats make sense.	Choose one or more. If more than one, designate a primary audience.	Choose one or more. If more than one, designate a primary purpose.	Choose several. Longer pieces will require more varied approaches.
The student takes on a role and writes from this perspective.	The final version must be published in exactly this format.	This is the student's intended audience. This is to whom the piece is being written.	This is why the piece is being written. The writer works toward achieving this goal.	This is how the writer will go about achieving his or her purpose.
• Advertiser • Newscaster • Tour Guide • Curator • Panelist • Reporter • Product Designer • Artist • Biographer • Political Candidate • Biologist • Engineer • Historian • Expert in ... • Parent • Teacher • Self • Detective • Editor	• Magazine Article • Editorial • Brochure • Short Story • Play • Fairy Tale • Myth • Poem • Novel • Report • Diary • Journal • Biography • Autobiography • Newspaper Article • Letter • Booklet • Interview • Textbook	• Friends • Parent • Self • Teacher • Young Students • Public Figures • Persons in Authority • Supervisor • General Public • People From Other Cultures • People From Other Time Periods • Professionals in Same Discipline • Investor • Judge or Jury • School Board	• Change Thinking • Inform • Explain • Change Action • Entertain • Initiate Thinking • Tell a Story • Instruct • Initiate Action	• Analyze • Challenge • Classify • Compare • Conclude • Contrast • Defend • Define • Demonstrate • Describe • Evaluate • Explain • Interpret • Investigate • Justify • Persuade • Predict • Propose • Question • Reflect

Sample Formal Assignment

To create a formal writing assignment, students simply follow the plan, making choices from each of the columns. Figure 5.4 shows three examples in the content areas of social studies, science, and mathematics.

Figure 5.4 Sample Formal Assignments

Content Area	Assignment
Social Studies	You are a newspaper reporter from the *Atlanta Constitution* covering the battle of Gettysburg. You have followed the battle and have now just listened to Lincoln's Gettysburg Address. Write a newspaper article for the people of Atlanta that will inform them of the results of the battle and its impact on the Confederate war effort. Describe the battle and its aftermath. Analyze the balance of power between the two sides as a result of the battle. Reflect on the sentiments of Unionists before and after Lincoln's speech.
Science	You are a biologist hired as a consultant to The Nature Conservancy. Create a brochure for the general public that explains the Greenhouse Effect and its impact on worldwide climatic conditions. Analyze current data on the effects of greenhouse gases and predict the consequences of widespread global warming. Propose alternatives to improve the situation that are consistent with current positions held by The Nature Conservancy.
Mathematics	You are an expert in fractions. Create a chapter for a textbook to be used by fourth-grade students that will instruct them in adding, subtracting, multiplying, and dividing fractions. Include an introduction that justifies the instructional method you choose.

Using Poetry for Writing Across the Curriculum

Poetry can be used for writing in any content area at any grade level. Students start reading and enjoying poetry in preschool and can be introduced to forms such as acrostic poems as a model for writing poetry as early as kindergarten. By eighth grade, students may be reading both classic and contemporary poets, such as Emily Dickinson and Maya Angelou.

Nancie Atwell (1998) makes the reading and writing connection explicit when introducing teachers to writing poetry. "My students started to write good poetry when they started to read good poetry, learned how to walk around inside it, learned that they wanted to walk around inside it…. Each year, students become accomplished poets, but first they become accomplished readers of poetry who have observed what the genre is good for and what it might do for them" (427). The same could be said with writing in any content area. For example, students may be introduced to science, technology, engineering, and mathematics in preschool and kindergarten through exploration and play. In Atwell's words, they learn "to walk around inside" these disciplines as writers and *want* "to walk around inside" them. A science, engineering, or mathematics writer in kindergarten will spiral upward as a writer throughout the grades.

Students are inspired to write in the specific disciplines by reading mentor texts or examples of writing formats. As Atwell (1998) points out with poetry, locating these favorite readings is a place to start. She recommended that teachers who were intimidated or new to poetry start with collections such as *Writing Poems* (2011) by Robert Wallace, *An Introduction to Poetry* (2013) by X. J. Kennedy, *Knock at a Star: A Child's Introduction to Poetry* (1999) by I. J. Kennedy and Dorothy Kennedy, and *Writing Toward Home: Tales and Lessons to Find Your Way* (1995) by Georgia Heard. Atwell, whose work was in middle grades, also listened to the response of her students and brought back their favorite poems year after year: "A Bummer" by Michael Casey, "Nothing Can Stay" by Robert Frost, "Tecumseh" by Mary Oliver, and "Dog's Death" by John Updike (1998), to name a few of many (1998). Her knowledge of literature and keen attention to student response revved up the engine of her writing classroom. The poems she read every day were the fuel.

The same technique can be used for introducing kindergarten students to poetry writing. Before introducing kindergartens to acrostics—a simple form which uses a letter from the poem title for the first word, phrase, or sentence for each line—they read from collections of favorite acrostics such as *Animal Acrostics* by David Hammon. They talk about their favorite examples and model acrostics in shared writing. Students quickly adopt the form as their own, as is shown in the example below from one kindergartner about his favorite pet:

CAT

Cuddles with me

Ate a mouse

Tabby!

By fourth grade, we have shared from *Pizza, Pigs, and Poetry: How to Share a Poem* by Jack Prelutsky, *Kid's Poems: Teaching Third and Fourth Graders to Love Writing Poetry* by Regie Routman, *African Acrostics: A Word Edgewise* by Avis Harley, *Poetry for Young People: Robert Frost* by Gary Schmidt, and scores of others. We love poet Brog Bagert and his Muse Project (http://www.brodbagert.com/muse-project/) and the work of poet David Harrison, which opens doors for poetry writing in science, mathematics, and social studies, connecting language learning with early childhood content areas. Sixth graders have responded particularly well to mentor texts such as *Giant Children and School Fever* by Brod Bagert and had fun in writer's workshop with simple patterns such as quatrains, which use two couplets to make an AABB poetry form. Students should explore and use many poetry forms, such as the ones illustrated in Figures 5.5 and 5.6.

Figure 5.5 Sample Poetry Form 1

A Cache of Poetry

There are many forms of poetry.

Couplet Two rhyming lines of verse	In the wintertime we go Walking through the fields of snow
Limerick Nonsense poem with 5 lines 1st, 2nd, and 5th lines rhyme	There once was a cow on the moon, Who traveled in the month of June. He mooed all night, And looked such a sight, As he continued to moo his tune.
Five W's Poetry Line 1: Who? Line 2: What? Line 3: Where? Line 4: When? Line 5: Why?	I Love to watch football In Mountaineer Stadium, During home games, Because excitement makes me happy.
Triante (Triangle Poem) Line 1: title, 1 word Line 2: smell, 2 words Line 3: touch/taste, 3 words Line 4: sight, 4 words Line 5: sound/action, 5 words	Ocean Clean, Fresh Salty, Wet, Cool Green, Murky, Wide, Deep Swell, Roll, Crash, Pound, Splash

Your Turn:

Chose one form of poetry from above, and write a poem.

(Gentry, McNeel, and Wallace-Nesler 2012 e)

Figure 5.6 Sample Poetry Form 2

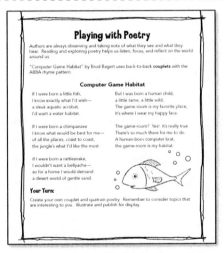

Playing with Poetry

Authors are always observing and taking note of what they see and what they hear. Reading and exploring poetry helps us listen, focus, and reflect on the world around us.

"Computer Game Habitat" by Brod Bagert uses back-to-back **couplets** with the ABBA rhyme pattern.

Computer Game Habitat

If I were born a little fish,
I know exactly what I'd wish—
a sleek aquatic acrobat,
I'd want a water habitat.

If I were born a chimpanzee
I know what would be best for me—
of all the places, coast to coast,
the jungle's what I'd like the most.

If I were born a rattlesnake,
I wouldn't want a bellyache—
so for a home I would demand
a desert world of gentle sand.

But I was born a human child,
a little tame, a little wild,
The game-room is my favorite place,
It's where I wear my happy face.

The game-room? Yes! It's really true.
There's so much there for me to do.
A human-born computer brat,
the game-room is my habitat.

Your Turn:

Create your own couplet and quatrain poetry. Remember to consider topics that are interesting to you. Illustrate and publish for display.

(Gentry, McNeel, and Wallace-Nesler 2013 g)

When Writing Across the Curriculum, remember that no matter what the discipline, poetry is a great format for writing and using words and concepts specific to the discipline. Create opportunities for students to do casual, semiformal, and formal writing in the content areas because all three types of writing encourage closer reading, lead to deeper inquiry, and ultimately lead to deeper thinking, comprehension, and understanding. These writing tasks will enhance students' abilities to have a voice of their own and be independent thinkers and writers. Writing Across the Curriculum not only stimulates students but also makes teaching in the disciplines more creative and stimulates us as teachers. No matter what subjects or disciplines you teach, these tips for writing across the curriculum will serve you well.

Tips for Writing Across the Curriculum

1. Show students good examples of writing in your discipline.

2. Model for students to show them what you want them to do.

3. Recognize that good writing takes time.

4. Embrace everyday writing ranging from short and informal activities to elaborate inquiry/writing projects that potentially take weeks or even months.

5. Include casual, semiformal, and formal writing across the curriculum.

6. Adopt the process-writing approach along with traits of quality writing.

7. Make writing assignments authentic and meaningful.

8. Consider occasional class time when the content-area period is structured for writer's workshop so that students are working on major content-area writing projects together.

9. Make sure that writers have an audience besides you, the teacher.

10. Encourage writers in your content area to share and interact with each piece of writing.

11. Avoid too many markups, and do not grade low-stakes pieces.

12. Compliment often to build students' confidence as you show what they are doing well and help them fix problems.

13. Don't forget feelings! Have you ever heard someone say, "I wish I could write that?" Almost everyone, including students, want to write. In order to become a writer, they must be invested in the process, and you must not forget their feelings. Make them feel good about writing by giving them authentic opportunities for publication even if it's as simple as a classroom magazine. Once they are published, they will say, "Hey, I'm a writer!" It's a good feeling.

Reflect and Review

1. What writing strategies are you currently using across the curriculum? How might you expand on that current instruction?

2. How can you plan a three-week unit based on the Justin Minkel model?

3. How can you use the following guidelines to plan a content-area writing project?

- Start with some easy casual writing activities on a daily or every other day basis.

- Gradually work to two or three more elaborate pieces per month.

- Engage students in a large formal writing project over six to eight weeks.

- Use chart in Figure 5.3 to plan the formal piece.

Chapter 6

Developing the Traits of Good Writing

"Language is empowering. Writer's language opens doors for students and changes their thinking forever. It gives them independence."

—Vicki Spandel (2008, x)

Speaking a Common Language

We recognize the traits of writing as the language of our writer's workshop. Vicki Spandel (2008) refers to the traits as "a writer's vocabulary for thinking, speaking, and working like writers" (6). During mini-lessons, partner conversations, conferences, and sharing, the traits are the common vocabulary for teaching and talking about writing. The aim is that the language of the traits transfers across content areas and grade levels, building school-wide continuity in the expectations of quality writing. Imagine if students, teachers, administrators, and parents fully understood and spoke the same language about writing. Even the youngest of writers would begin to recognize and understand those quality characteristics undeniably present in the texts of their fellow writers or in the books of their favorite authors.

The traits of quality writing were identified in 1984 through research projects conducted by teachers searching for an answer to the question *What makes good writing work?* They read and analyzed writing, dedicating their efforts toward developing a simple means of writing assessment for teachers and students. These studies at the Northwest Regional Educational Laboratory, now recognized as Education Northwest, identified the following attributes essential for good writing:

As we teach writing mini-lessons, collaborate with partners, and develop our writing skills, the traits serve as the core of students' learning. The complex writing process becomes more accessible when students are taught these quality writing traits, writing strategies for developing each of those traits, and a method of using the traits as an objective measure for assessing writing. When we use the language of the traits of writing, we build a community of writers that values writing and sees its members as authors of important work.

Ideas

"The topics to write about are as countless as the stars. I believe that the best ideas live inside of us. It's our job to dig them out."

—Ralph Fletcher (2000, 15)

110

All writing, from children's picture books to political speeches, begins with an idea. The trait of ideas is often referred to as the "heart" of the message. That idea flows into the writer's theme and is supported by well-developed details that interest, inform, excite, and entertain the reader. This trait not only focuses on establishing the main idea of the writing but also creates descriptive, precise details that pull the audience into the writing. To support students in the development of the trait of ideas, teach them the following skills:

- **Focus on an idea:** What do I want to write about?

- **Zero in on and narrow the idea:** Is my topic specific and manageable?

- **Expand and explain to develop the idea:** Do I have knowledge and/or experience to add anecdotes and details?

Too often, students have the unmistakable notion that they do not have anything to write about. They think if they have not climbed Mount Everest or visited a famous theme park, their ideas are not worthy of a manuscript. In addition, students sometimes appear in our classrooms having been fed writing prompts in previous grades and lack the experience of developing ideas on their own. We need to show our students how to observe details, notice the world around them, take note of the unusual, listen for topics that interest them, and "see the world as writers." It is through our teaching that students will become successful in selecting and developing the trait of ideas.

How to Teach Ideas

Provide numerous opportunities for students to choose their own topics for writing. When students select topics, their writing is often full of conviction, passion, and voice. Young writers can develop confidence in their writing when they are interested in and have knowledge of the topics about which they are writing. Eventually, students see themselves as writers and recognize writing as a personal life skill rather than a teacher assignment.

Modeling and demonstrating how to create a list of topics for writing is the first step in developing the trait of ideas. Begin by creating an "Expert List" of things we are knowledgeable about and care to share with the class. "Think aloud" as each idea is considered and then dismissed or added to the list, sharing briefly why that topic might be a good idea for writing. Next, after students discuss topics they might write about, create a class chart of *Topics We Can Write About*. This cumulative chart includes writing ideas that many of them have in common, like brothers and sisters, pets, grandparents, sports, and subject matter the class studied. The idea list, along with the group list, will initiate writing ideas for students as they create their own open-ended list of topics for writing. Scaffold and guide students through this process to ensure that students have a clear understanding of the task and the support necessary to succeed.

What is most important in the teaching of ideas is that students are helped to recognize that writing topics are all around them. Writing ideas are found in the following:

- **Family stories:** Encourage students to talk to family members about topics for their writing, such as family traditions, special memories from a younger age, trips and vacations, and family members.

- **The arts:** Use art, music and lyrics, photographs, poetry, and dance to inspire ideas for writing. Every picture tells a story, and using pictures from magazines, books, advertisements, family photos, the newspaper, and the Internet can all inspire ideas for writing. Shel Silverstein's poem "One Sister For Sale" is an excellent example of poetry that generates writing ideas.

- **Classmates:** Through partner discussions and sharing opportunities, writing ideas are sparked. When Gabbie shares her writing idea of getting ice cream with her grandmother after school on Fridays, Jose recalls how when he got ice cream and his little sister's ice cream fell off the cone, she sat down on the sidewalk and started eating it. Sharing starts the brain thinking, "Oh, that reminds me of...."

- **Books:** Share literature from different genres for many reasons. As we share fiction and nonfiction, topics are explored and added to a student's list of writing ideas. When reading with a class, think aloud about how a sentence, phrase, or picture sparks a memory and how to write about that memory.

- **Questions:** What do we wonder about? What do we want to know more about? These are topics that motivate students to research, explore, and write. Writing ideas based on questions can also create a strong voice, particularly when the writer develops passion about the topic (e.g., coal vs. wind turbines).

- **Ourselves:** The people we know, the places we go, the things we treasure, the activities we enjoy, the things we like or dislike, and the everyday stuff are all writing ideas just waiting to be molded into some form of writing.

Once students collect ideas and begin using them for their writing, help them zoom in on and narrow that idea into a focused topic. It is not uncommon for students to select broad topics that leave them overwhelmed with the amount of information or lead to vague writing of "sunrise to sunset" adventures. One of the best ways to narrow the topic with young students is a visual representation of what Calkins and Martinelli (2006) refer to as the "watermelon to seed" topics, and we name "story seeds." The process is to use the body and hands or picture cards to represent the broad topic—football (the watermelon). Next, cut the melon in half and narrow in on the idea—playing football (half watermelon). Continue to narrow that topic—my team and coach (slices of the watermelon). From that, we find story seed(s)—lessons my coach taught me about life or the winning touchdown (watermelon seeds). Refer to Figure 3.1 in Chapter 3.

Another successful approach to teach students to narrow ideas into more manageable topics is to ask questions: *who, what, where, why, when,* and *how.* The following is a nonfiction example.

- **What do I know or care about?**—bullying

- **When?**—bullying during the middle school years

- **Where?**—at school or after school

- **How?**—using social media to bully in middle school

- **Who?**—middle school girls using social media to bully (Focused writing idea)

Students often have difficulty on standardized writing assessment prompts because their writing lacks in idea development. Their essays may be short, with only a few related details. Mini-lessons should support writers in developing details that are interesting, unique, and informative. Details "show" what is happening and don't just tell about the event, and details should hold the reader's attention.

Students can usually add unique anecdotes and interesting details by simply asking, "Why?" If you have ever been around a toddler who asks a simple question, you can relate to this thinking. You respond with a simple reply, only to hear another "Why?" During this little conversation exchange, you provide information—details for the toddler's story. It may not be written down, but those details are stored and added to that child's knowledge base to be used another time. Other question words will produce some details, but "Why" can manufacture an endless supply.

Drawings, pictures, and webs are used frequently to teach idea development. After the process of selecting and narrowing a writing idea is modeled, we often begin building a sketch of the story. Each object in the sketch becomes a writing detail in a simple beginning, middle, and end storyboard sketch. Even the youngest writers can find details in the colors, sizes, names, and labels they add to their drawings. Pictures and postcards can serve as a resource for students to practice developing details from ideas. Teaching students to be specific, when giving details, will enhance their writing. For example, students may say they see trees in the picture. More specifically, they see "the 3,500-year-old Sequoia." Students can also use their senses to write what they see, hear, smell, feel, and taste when "looking into" the picture.

Model and share several examples of ideas developed with authentic texts from favorite authors, your writing, and student writing samples. Students need multiple modeled mini-lessons, a variety of strategies, and opportunities for practice before applying the strategies successfully in their own writing. Creating a class anchor chart with modeled strategies is a valuable resource for supporting developing writers.

Types of Lessons to Teach Ideas

Figure 6.1 shows an additional lesson idea used when teaching students to collect writing ideas. Sharing and modeling lists of our favorites typically sparks numerous writing ideas for students to add to their own lists and has many possible avenues to explore (e.g, favorite people, places, foods, and winter activities). Consider lists of things that are not favorites, such as things that make you sad or angry, or the worst days. The ideas on these lists may be broad initially, but they can be narrowed once students become more confident in their writing.

You can even create an alphabet idea board that can be expanded throughout the year. If space is limited in the classroom, take it into the hallway and inspire other teachers and students with your class's writing ideas. Each letter has its own page or box, and ideas can simply be written in or added with sticky notes. For example, as students expand their knowledge of bats in reading/science, add *bats* to the B section of the board. Provide students with individual alphabet charts so they may add their own ideas for writing. They can be familiar topics or new ideas for exploration.

Figure 6.1 Sample Alphabet Idea Board

Ideas from A to Z

Authors often get their writing topics from their own personal experiences. They may record topics and ideas that they want to learn about and explore so they may share information, concepts, and opinions. Here are a few topics to get you started:

Aa animal habitats	Bb bullying	Cc China	Dd deserts
Ee environments	Ff friendship	Gg grandparents	Hh healthy habits
Ii iguanas	Jj juggling	Kk kites	Ll lunar eclipse
Mm migration	Nn natural resources	Oo Olympics	Pp planets
Qq quilts	Rr Rembrandt	Ss sailing	Tt Texas
Uu uniforms	Vv vacations	Ww Walt Disney	Xx X-rays
Yy yo-yo	Zz zodiac		

Your Turn:

Begin developing your Ideas from A to Z list for writing in your Writer's Notebook. Remember, you can revisit and add topics to this list throughout the year. Your topics should include ideas for informative, opinion/argumentative, and narrative writing.

(Gentry, McNeel, and Wallace-Nesler 2013 g)

Use texts to support students as they generate, narrow, and develop ideas. We often think of mentor text as literature from our favorite authors, but they may also include newspaper articles with interesting leads, brochures full of details, Internet blogs with writing samples, and even student writing examples. Telling students about using sensory details, prepositional phrases, dialogue, and similes is not nearly as effective as showing them how these strategies are used in authentic text. Using the text *All About Rattlesnakes* by Jim Arnosky (2002) is one example to teach narrowing the topic. It is not just about animals, reptiles, or snakes. Instead, it provides specific information about that unique type of snake.

Asking questions not only supports writers as they narrow topics but can also spark ideas for writing and expand idea development. Asking questions like *Who/What do I know a lot about?*, *Where have I been or do I want to go?*, or *How do astronauts brush their teeth?* all create possible writing ideas. We also like to use "I Wonder" questions to narrow topic choice and/or to expand details, as shown in Figure 6.2.

Figure 6.2 Sample I Wonder List

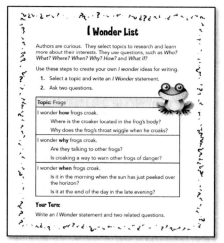

(Gentry, McNeel, and Wallace-Nesler 2013 e)

Modeling methods for students to add details to their drafts is not only a strategy for revision but also a means for developing ideas without rewriting the draft. Adding "spider legs" on a strip(s) of paper stapled or taped to the top or bottom of the draft provides the space needed to add small details. To add more information, attach a page to each side of the draft to develop the story idea about what happened before and after. Another technique students really enjoy is "story surgery," where they cut their story apart and staple or "stitch in" an additional paper section used to write more information (you can use tape and draw stitches).

Use magnifying glasses, binoculars, cameras, video recorders, or phones to introduce students to developing ideas. Helping students understand that they only need to zoom in or stop the moment to generate details is a valuable writing strategy. Consider showing snapshots and asking questions such as *What is happening in that moment?* or *If we moved in slow motion, what would we notice, hear, and smell?* Encourage students to use their senses when expanding details. Have students create a camera lens by cutting a circle in a notecard or piece of paper. Peek through the "lens" to take a snapshot and generate a list of details, or create a mental image of one small part of a memory and explode it into ideas and details for a story.

Questions to Use When Conferencing about Ideas

It is important to listen to students. Then, guide them through questioning. Writing conferences should be student centered with open-ended questions that nudge the writer forward. While every conference is a different conversation, these are comment and question examples that can be used when conferring with students about ideas.

- What do you enjoy doing?

- What/Who do you care about?

- What do you think you might like to write about today?

- What ideas did you explore from our classroom list or your personal lists?

- What is the main idea of your writing today?

- You know a lot about your topic_____. Do you have a favorite_____?

- Tell me more about …

- You focused on your idea! I want to know more. Can you describe…?

- Can you add details or an example to clarify what you mean here?

- How can you use your senses to add descriptive details for your reader?

- What interesting details or facts might readers be surprised to learn?

- This is a unique topic! Everyone may not be familiar with the topic, so where might your reader need more clarification or explanation?

Suggestions for Teaching Ideas

What do we do when a student gets stuck and just cannot come up with ideas for writing? Praise and encourage! Praise the student for previous ideas developed in their writing and encourage them to explore other possible ideas by looking through books, magazines, newspapers, talking to their writing partner, or simply closing their eyes and thinking about the events of the past few days.

When student-writing ideas become repetitious or lacking in substance, combine partners or small groups and brainstorm writing ideas with an idea web. Share the webs with the class, and have students add ideas to their personal lists. The collaboration and sharing is sure to spark new and interesting ideas. Encourage writers to be aware of the "happenings" in their lives. Writing ideas are often generated through conversations and the simple question, "What's up?" Students can create a list of "what's up?" topics related to what is currently happening, such as the following:

- **At school:** soccer tournament, spirit week, lunch
- **In class:** new student, test, current topics in science and social studies
- **At home:** a new pet, visiting grandma, baking cookies, swimming lessons
- **In the news:** current government topic, latest fad, weather conditions

There is great value in sharing and providing a variety of genres and texts by authors you and your students admire. Literature provides a plethora of writing topics. The subjects in the text, the personal connections, and the genre easily evoke writing ideas. Just one book may spark a number of writing topics for a student. Take time to model thinking when making connections to writing ideas during read alouds. Quickly jot down class writing ideas on a chart and allow students a minute to add topics to their own ideas lists.

A topic we cannot avoid and are asked about often is giving students writing prompts. We want our writer's workshop to be student-centered and our students to become independent writers. Consistently providing prompts for writing creates a teacher-centered classroom and makes students dependent on the teacher for always choosing a topic to write about. When students select their own personal ideas for writing, they are more confident, knowledgeable, and enthusiastic and thus produce better writing. It is recommended to give writing prompts when practicing a specific skill and when preparing for writing assessments. It is important to do some "test prep" to make sure students know what to expect when they are required to use prompts on high-stakes tests, but prompts should not be made the focus of the writing program.

Be positive in your comments when discussing ideas. The words you say and how you say them can encourage a writer to move forward with confidence and develop an eagerness to succeed.

Organization

> "It is organization that gives direction to our writing. It is the internal structure of a piece and provides the backbone to which all the pieces are connected."
> —Northwest Regional Educational Laboratory (2005, 245)

When a piece of writing is well organized, it flows so smoothly that the reader often loses track of time while fully comprehending the text. Text with clear, logical organization enriches and showcases the idea or theme of the writing. The trait of organization involves the structure and order of the writer's ideas and the transition from one idea to the next. Within that structure lies an interesting and inviting introduction, a well thought out sequence of ideas and supporting details in the middle, transitions that connect all the pieces together, and a conclusion that leaves the reader content yet a bit reflective about the theme of the writing.

Letters, newspaper articles, poetry, essays, and lab reports all have a logical framework that is selected based on the content and purpose of writing. These frameworks are writing patterns that guide readers logically through the text. Readers expect and depend on these organizational patterns to make sense of the information they read. When patterns are illogical or inconsistent, the reader becomes confused and disinterested, and comprehension of material is often lost. The organizational structure affects how readers interpret ideas.

Determining the pattern of organization is an important decision based on the topic, audience, and purpose of the writing. There are a number of patterns, also referred to as text structures, as well as supportive transitional words and phrases from which writers select when planning their ideas, information, and insights.

The following are a few common text structures authors frequently use in narrative, informational, and argumentative text.

Sequence or Chronological: In this type of text, events or items are listed in a specific order or in a list of procedural steps. The sequence is important to the meaning of the context.

Compare and Contrast: This structure features the similarities (comparisons) and differences (contrast) the author makes between two or more things.

Cause and Effect: In this pattern, the author presents a cause (the action) and shares the effects (outcomes) of that action.

Problem and Solution: This text presents one or more problems and explains how the problem(s) can be solved or have already been solved. It may also include the effects of the solutions.

Description: This type of text structure describes a person, idea, place, or event by listing characteristics, descriptions, and examples to create a mental image.

Understanding and recognizing these organizational patterns not only support our students as writers by structuring and developing their ideas, but it also helps them as readers to follow an author's ideas more easily and improve their understanding of the meaning of the text.

How to Teach Organization

When thinking of the organization of writing, a complex text structure reserved for "older" students often is first in our thoughts. However, the simple acts of adding a title and *The End* tell us that a young writer recognizes the need for a beginning and end to be included in his or her writing. Therefore, we want to be mindful of the developmental levels of our writers and recognize their efforts while further developing the trait. Our goal when teaching the trait of organization is to provide mini-lessons that show students how to create inviting introductions, writing structures to guide and support the reader, transition words to signal the reader, and an ending that wraps things up.

What's In the Beginning?

In this paper, I will tell you about.... The Civil War is the topic of my.... These overly broad and boring lead statements will have an audience losing interest before even getting started. With the plethora of reading material, TV shows, and Internet media, the first few sentences or moments are critical in the success of maintaining the audience. Writers need to be supported as they create introductions that capture the reader's attention and entice them to continue reading the rest of the text. Creating the "just right" lead sentence can be difficult, and students begin to feel defeated before they even get started. Remind them that many authors leave the first sentence until later and encourage them to move on and return to the hook sentence at a later time. Sharing examples from literature and student samples is an excellent method of exposing students to quality leads, such as beginning with a question, quote, onomatopoeia, dialogue, an interesting fact, simile, or metaphor, to name a few. Students should also explore texts and media independently to find examples of quality leads as well as nonexamples to share in class or display on a chart as a resource. Besides the hook, students should explore the introductory paragraph that establishes the purpose of the writing for the reader. This often includes sharing the characters and setting in narrative writing or the topic or argument in expository writing.

What's In the Middle?

In the middle, we find all the ideas logically grouped into different parts or paragraphs that keep the reader engaged in the writing. There is no magic formula to follow when selecting an organizational pattern for writing, and there are a number of structures that can be used and combined when organizing the same information. Provide support to students through sharing text examples and graphic organizers that represent text structures of different genres. A variety of graphic organizers should serve as foundational support for developing writers, but this resource should be removed to allow students to grow as writers. Be careful not to overuse the same organizer. This can produce "formula" writing that is trite and uninteresting. Figure 6.3 shows examples and recommended graphic organizers that complement each of the text structures previously mentioned.

Figure 6.3 Sample Graphic Organizers that Represent Text Structures

Text Structure	Graphic Organizer	Example
Sequence or Chronological Storyboard/Sequence Chain/Timeline This can be easily adapted for younger writers, with simple beginning/middle/end or made more complex to challenge students.	1 → 2 → 3 4 → 5 → 6 7 → 8 → 9	Students enjoy writing personal narratives. Storyboards help organize their ideas and details. *How things happen*, such as how a star is formed or how food is digested and *how-to* topics like brushing your teeth or harvesting grapes are possible topics for sequence chains.
Compare and Contrast Venn Diagram Venn Diagrams visually represent attributes that are similar in the overlapping area and different in individual circles.	(Venn Diagram: two overlapping circles)	Venn Diagrams may be used when identifying similarities and differences between animals such as a lion and tiger or two presidents. Often, consumer reports compare and contrast different product brands to inform the public.
Cause and Effect Event-Cause or T-chart Either chart serves to support students in planning writing.	Effect/Event Cause Cause Cause Cause | Effect	Changes in weather patterns (causes) may explain the unexpected hurricane (effect/event), or the hurricane (effect/event) could be explained as the cause of a number of hardships.
Problem and Solution Flow Chart A simple flow chart can support writers of different developmental levels by simply increasing or decreasing the number of events in the organizer.	Problem ↓ Event ↓ Event ↓ Event ↓ Solution	Problem and solution can be used to persuade the reader that motorized transportation is a problem, offering alternatives and then recommending solutions like riding a bike. Younger writers can relate to mentor texts such as *Knuffle Bunny* when identifying the problem (lost the bunny) and solution (had to backtrack), and then create their own writing.

Text Structure	Graphic Organizer	Example
Description detail web/sensory web Topic is in the center and descriptive details are listed in each circle. Additional stems may branch to represent more related details.	(detail web with "Topic" in center circle and connecting circles)	A book about Italy (main topic) and the culture, people, and land (subtopics) is an example of a detail web. The subtopics would then each contain details represented by additional web lines. Brochures often contain examples of descriptive writing.

Besides graphic organizers, we must also inform students of text features that enhance the organization of writing. Authors use text features to bring attention to important details and guide their reader through the text. Encourage students to notice text features in literature as well as media sources, and talk about the purpose of the feature. Generate a class chart or have students add a list of features to their folders and notebooks that they would like to try in their writing. Some text features to share with students are shown in Figure 6.4.

Figure 6.4 Sample Text Features

Fiction	Nonfiction	
Title	Title	Labels
Chapter	Table of contents	Graphics
Index	Index	Maps
Illustrations	Photos	Diagrams
Bold Print	Captions	Font
Continuous Text	Glossary	Bold
Paragraphing	Date line	Color
Dialogue	Headings	Italics
	Sub-title	Cut away

Transition words and phrases are often referred to as signal words because they direct the reader through the author's thoughts. These words are selected carefully and serve as valuable tools that connect the writer's ideas, words, sentences, and paragraphs in a cohesive manner. Transitional words and phrases are used to summarize, conclude, and elaborate, and indicate time order, contrast, comparison, and cause and effect. Teaching students to recognize signal words in text provides authentic examples that will help them when developing the organizational structure in their own writing.

Specific words and phrases are linked to particular text structures. A few examples are as follows:

Sequence or Chronological: after, as soon as, before, in the beginning, during, first, immediately, next, not long after, then, when, finally, while, as, earlier, later, today, in the end, meanwhile

Compare and Contrast: (for similarities) also, additionally, just as, as if, as though, as well as, like, and similarly; (for differences) but, different, unlike, yet, only, although, whereas, in contrast, conversely, compared to, however, on the other hand, rather

Cause and Effect: because, since, for, furthermore, so, as a result, consequently, otherwise, thus, without a doubt, the major reason, of major concern

Problem and Solution: as a result, consequently, beginning with, effects of, finally, for this reason, may be due to, if … then, when … then, in order to, leads to/led to, therefore

Description: above, appears to be, beside, between, looks like, outside, over, just like, under, for example, for instance

What's In the End?

Sometimes students just do not know how and when to finish their writing, so they resort to clichés such as *And then I woke up!*, *The End*, and *That's all folks!* Those writing conclusions should raise the "time for a mini-lesson" antennae for a teacher. There are a number of ways to teach students to conclude their writing, but the main idea we want students to learn is that the kind of ending is determined by the author's purpose. When writing to entertain, ask yourself if you want the reader to smile, giggle a bit, be surprised, feel our joy or sadness, loop right back to our beginnings, or think deeply. Students need to become aware of conclusions of expository texts meant to inform or persuade the reader, such as restating the main idea, summarizing the key points, and using questions to entice the reader to learn more or consider a point of view. Let students know that most authors write and rewrite their endings many times before settling on a final conclusion. One of the most successful methods used to support students when writing endings is to explore the conclusions of many authors.

We encourage you to read to your students, no matter their age, simply for the joy of reading. Exposing students to language, leads, text structures, vocabulary, and endings is never time wasted in a classroom. After the reading, stop and discuss the organizational pattern used by the author and why that structure was chosen over another. Complete an outline or graphic organizer of the text, and search for signal words associated with the text structure together. Then, complete one in small groups. Soon, students will begin to read like a writer, developing an awareness of the author's use of leads, text structure, signal words, and endings. However, creating a beginning, middle, and end are only the beginning points in developing the trait of organization. Providing support and guidance as developing writers explore new techniques, along with cheers of encouragement, is sure to enhance the structure of students' writing.

Types of Lessons to Teach Organization

There are a multitude of mini-lessons that can be taught that support students in developing the trait of organization. For example, model and share examples of different leads, text structures, and endings from favorite literature, and provide a variety of texts from different genres and send partners on a scavenger or treasure hunt to find examples. Record and display strong examples and discuss what makes them good examples.

You can also have students rewrite the introduction or ending to a favorite fairy tale. Be sure to model and discuss specific examples before asking students to experiment. Begin with a few possibilities, and add additional lead and ending examples as students develop as writers and become more aware of the importance of audience and purpose. It is fun to play "Guess My Lead" or "Who's Ending Is This Anyway?" and have the student-created hook/ending read or displayed. Then, have classmates try to determine which fairy tale it matches as seen in Figure 6.5.

Figure 6.5 Sample Fairy Tale Story Organization

(Gentry, McNeel, and Wallace-Nesler 2012 d)

Support students by providing scaffold instruction and thinking aloud during modeled demonstrations. With young writers, start small by modeling just a sentence and then a paragraph that uses a specific text structure. Try using the same topic to show students the different ways to present text. Also provide opportunities for sequencing activities to help students see the value of ordering thoughts and ideas. You can begin by showing younger writers three to five sequencing cards and ask them to create a story by arranging them in a logical order. Later, ask writers to add one or two sentences to represent each card. Introduce a few transition words and have students determine their order. Students enjoy making a game out of schoolwork. Simply add a game title like "Order, Order in the Classroom" and enjoy as students arrange four or five short sentences or paragraphs into writing that makes sense. Provide short stories, newspaper articles, and recipes, or have students bring in their own examples (be sure to preview before sharing) to use for the activity.

Teach students that TAP can help them develop their writing plan. *T* refers to the *type* of text such as an article, a story, or letter. *A* represents the reading *audience*, and *P* is the *purpose* of the writing such as to entertain, inform, and persuade. These elements provide information to support decisions about the organizational structure of the writing.

Many early writing text structures are associated with expository writing. However, narrative writing often contains combinations of different text structures. For example, a story is told through a sequential pattern. The characters encounter a problem and find a solution before the story ends. Writers are often taught to recognize the literary elements of fiction first through sharing literature from favorite authors, and then they are introduced to storyboards and sequence chains to support their efforts of developing characters, creating the setting, identifying the problem through careful pacing, and then solving the problem. Figure 6.6 shows an example of an organizer used to develop characters in a story, while Figure 6.7 illustrates a plot map.

Figure 6.6 Sample Character Development Organizer

Build-a-Character

Memorable characters are those that the reader gets to know well. They have traits that are believable and invite the reader into the story.

Character: Templeton the Rat from *Charlotte's Web*	
Appearance: a chubby rat, long tail, sharp teeth for gnawing, claws for clutching food	**Revealed by:** After his night at the fair he has swollen double his size. Later, he agrees to trade for food so he can become fatter and bigger than all the other rats.
Personality: sneaky, thoughtless, unkind, ill-tempered	**Revealed by:** He creeps up to the goslings, close to the wall. He snickers when Wilbur falls, takes his food, and bites his tail.
Likes/Dislikes: Likes being alone, food Dislikes being bothered	**Revealed by:** When Wilbur wants him to play, Templeton says, "…I never do those things if I can avoid them…I prefer to spend my time eating, gnawing, spying and hiding. I am a glutton not a merry-maker."
Relationship to others: He can do without them, but they continue to ask him for help even though they have to bribe him with food.	**Revealed by:** Each time he is asked to retrieve words for Charlotte, he ends up with something in return.

Your Turn:
Create and illustrate your character, then write a description of your character that includes the four character traits listed in this notebook entry. Just for fun, create a character cinquain!

(Gentry, McNeel, and Wallace-Nesler 2012 d)

Figure 6.7 Sample Plot Map

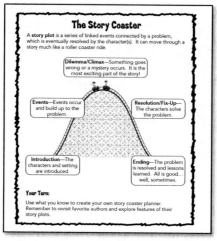

(Gentry, McNeel, and Wallace-Nesler 2012 f)

Start small when introducing transition words. Begin by modeling how to connect two sentences together using transition words. Incorporate different words within the same sentences to stress how the words affect the meaning. Then provide sentences and transition words for students, and allow time for them to explore possibilities. After students practice with sentences, model a similar process with paragraphs. Next, move to short articles from the newspaper or magazine. Black out any transition/signal words in the article, and then have students complete it to create a logical story. As students share, discuss and be amazed at some of the choices and how the meaning is altered based on those choices. Be careful when teaching students to add transition words in their writing. It is usually present on the standardized writing assessment rubrics, and therefore students need to be aware of how to meet those requirements. Yet when writing is organized into a systematic and logical order, there may not be a need to include transition words that might take away from the flow of the text. Teach students to use them when they want to "signal" to the reader, as shown in Figure 6.8.

Figure 6.8 Sample Transitional Signals

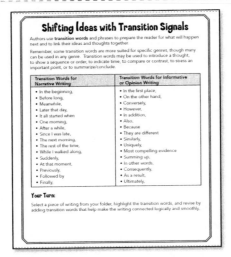

(Gentry, McNeel, and Wallace-Nesler 2012 g)

Questions to Use When Conferring about Organization

Talk with even the youngest students as writers about what makes good writing. Ask questions, listen closely, and simply have a conversation about what is important to this writer at this moment. Use the following questions to guide your conversations about organization.

- What type of text are you writing today?
- For whom are you writing? Why did you direct your writing to that audience?
- What is the purpose of your writing piece today?
- How does your lead grab the reader's attention?
- What happened right before…? What happened right after…?
- Do all your ideas have a common connection?
- How might you make this part clearer for the reader?
- What signal word might help connect your ideas here?
- How might the order of your ideas be arranged?

- How would a time line help the reader follow the sequence of your ideas?

- How does the organizational structure guide the reader through writing? Are there any sections that need further development or less information?

- How might you move your reader through the writing at a faster/slower pace here?

- How do you want your reader to react at the end of your writing?

- What do you want your reader to take away from your writing?

- How can you create an ending that...?

Literature to Support Teaching the Trait of Organization

Literature should be considered a valuable resource for writing instruction and particularly for building student awareness of the trait of organization. Some valuable texts used in organization mini-lessons are shown in Figure 6.9. Although highlighted in the trait of organization for features such as lead, ending, transition, and text structures, these can be used when exploring other traits. For example, *Owl Moon* by Jane Yolen can be explored for organization as well as for word choice as we examine the use of figurative language.

Figure 6.9 Sample Texts to Use in Organization Mini-Lessons

Organization Feature	Title
Lead	*Bedhead* by Margie Palatini *Grandpa's Teeth* by Rod Clement *Owl Moon* by Jane Yolen *Because of Winn Dixie* by Kate DiCamillo *Charlotte's Web* by E. B. White *My Dog, My Hero* by Betsy Byars, Betsy Duffey, and Laurie Myers
Sequence	*Lights! Camera! Action!* by Gail Gibbons *Castle* by David Macaulay *The Giving Tree* by Shel Silverstein
Cause and Effect	*Danger! Volcanoes* by Seymour Simon *The Bee Tree* by Patricia Polacco
Compare and Contrast	*We the People* by Peter Spier *Crocodiles and Alligators* by Seymour Simon
Problem and Solution	*Knuffle Bunny* by Mo Willems *If You Traveled on the Underground Railroad* by Ellen Levine
Description	*Owl Moon* by Jane Yolen *Twilight Comes Twice* by Ralph Fletcher
Transitions	*Garden of Abdul Gasazi* by Chris Van Allsburg *Centerburg Tales: More Adventures of Homer Price* by Robert McCloskey *Wilma Unlimited: How Wilma Randolph Became the World's Fastest Woman* by Kathleen Krull and David Diaz
Endings	*Fly Away Home* by Eve Bunting *Chicken Sunday* by Patricia Polacco *The Stranger* by Chris Van Allsburg *The Relatives Came* by Cynthia Rylant *Lily's Purple Plastic Purse* by Kevin Henkes

Voice

"Print is a silent language. Children want to give voice to their stories. They want their print to speak out loud."
—Lucy Calkins (Walshe 1982, 92)

When conducting workshops on scoring writing, we are often asked about what makes the difference between a writing paper that is "good" and a writing paper that is "excellent." Even though many districts do not include it as a rubric exemplar, we never hesitate to say, "Voice." When the writing draws you in, stirs your emotions, and you want to read more, you have made that personal connection with the writer's voice. A writing piece may be well organized with outstanding conventions, but without voice, it is lifeless and flat.

Voice is what makes a piece of writing personal, unique, and notable. Pulitzer prize-winning journalist and author of many books on the art of teaching writing, Donald Murray (2004), has called voice the person in the writing. The reader "hears" the writer's voice, which imparts the writer's unique personality or perception in a way that impacts the reader's feelings, understanding, or perspective. One student told us, "Voice is when the writer puts his or her personal thumbprint on a piece of writing and speaks to the reader in his or her own special way." It gives writing a punch, spark, or flair and keeps it from being mundane or dull. Voice shows feelings. Speech bubbles, a catchy combination of just the right words, the pace and inflection of the wording, alliteration or sound, or perhaps a well-placed exclamation point can give voice to even the earliest samples of young students' writing. As writers develop, their voices can become louder. They begin to recognize their audience, and use their point of view to influence the response of the reader in their writing.

Every piece of writing has voice or a lack of it. Voice can be strong, and the reader/writer can hear it, or it can be weak, bordering on silence. If a reader says, "That piece of writing doesn't speak to me," it likely has little voice. It is writing that brings a tear to our eye, a smile to our lips, and a chill down our spines that rings with voice. You know you have found voice when you can hardly wait to share the writing or literature with your students, colleagues, or friends. A writer's voice can be clear, cogent, logical, fun, hilarious, doleful, sad, provocative, foreboding, upsetting, scientific, historical, or lyrical. Good writers are always in search of the perfect voice for a piece of writing. Voice is what makes the print speak to the reader, tug at the heartstrings, or titillate the brain.

How to Teach Voice

Voice has been described as hard to define and difficult to teach (Elbow 1998; Graves 1983; Lensmire 1998; Sperling and Appleman 2011). It's true that voice is full of hard-to-describe elements. Think of teaching voice as like tending to a garden: first, planting the seeds through sharing and modeling a variety of examples and then waiting for a glimpse of the plant—a well-placed exclamation point or a story that evokes empathy or humor. We water and nurture the plants, recognizing and celebrating even the smallest of successes. Eventually, those plants will bloom, like the young authors. An author's true voice develops through practice with writing and maturity with life's experiences. Remember to always be on the lookout to spotlight a student's writing and/or illustrations with voice. Sometimes, students surprise us when they write with detailed voice about something on which they are an expert or are intensely passionate.

Teach voice with three goals in mind: finding and recognizing voice, matching voice to purpose, and developing individual voice. Begin by modeling voice with favorite authors. This can be done using a variety of genres, and it especially works well when you talk about the voice in your own favorite children's literature because the author has connected with you personally. It is important that students be exposed to strong examples that illustrate voice in a variety of genres. Comparing two pieces of art, such as a Picasso and a Van Gogh, and talking about what makes each unique helps students recognize the trait of voice. Music, advertisements, newspaper articles, TV programs, movies, and video games all have a distinctive voice that students can learn to recognize through style, genre, and even emotion. Voice is much more likely to be present when students begin to understand the process of matching voice to the purpose of their writing. The purpose may be relative to the audience or reader of the writing. For example, an essay on the adventures of visiting the beach may contain details, style, and emotion that are different from a note written to a best friend sharing the fun in the sun experience. The writing format also contributes to the purpose of writing. A letter, invitation, school report, newspaper article, journal entry, and an essay each has a distinct voice. The purpose of writing is evident in different genres such as narrative, informative, and argumentative. These different genres may inspire or require different voices.

Meeting the third goal, developing individual voice, is an ongoing instructional process and begins to develop as young writers become more confident and are provided opportunities for choice in their writing. When students write about meaningful topics, they share their passion with excited energy in their writing. Their writing is stronger because they have knowledge of the subject and understand the vocabulary related to the topic. When given choice, writers are more likely to readily express their emotions or tone in their writing.

Teach voice by creating lessons that focus on how students can connect with their readers and compel them to keep reading. Remember that an important consideration in teaching voice is to create a classroom environment that encourages students to speak out, explore, be creative, and share their personal perspective.

Types of Lessons to Teach Voice

Use a favorite mentor text such as *Alligator Baby* by Robert Munsch (2002) to show how Munsch writes in a humorous voice and uses unexpected twists and dialogue to create his hilarious story. A mentor text such as *Fly Away Home* by Eve Bunting (1993) can be shared by having students use emotion cards to identify and discuss how the author established voice in the literature. To do this, create emotions cards and ask students to prescribe emotions to characters or write so that the reader feels a targeted emotion. Remember not to use the emotion word in the writing! Instead of using such words as *happy, sad,* and *mad,* go beyond and use words such as *excited, dismal,* and *angry.*

A voice chart can also be created to develop a character. Write the following headings on the left side of the chart:

- **Mood:** What mood does the story have?
- **Personality:** How does the author show the reader the character's personality?

- **Thoughts:** What is the character thinking?

- **Senses:** What is the character seeing, hearing, smelling, and feeling?

- **Actions:** What actions reflect the character's personality? Does the character seem real to you?

Use music from different cultures and genres, such as "Peter and the Wolf" by Sergei Prokofiev, art by Van Gogh and Dorothea Lange, or poems from poets like Shel Silverstein and Langston Hughes to explore voice. In a two- or three-month Civil War unit, have students do wide reading of Civil War nonfiction, including biographies and a variety of Civil War topics and events. Exposure to voice in the literature they read surrounding this unit of study will help students create their own unique voice. Then have them read selections from informational text and contrast it with a short selection from good literature on the same topic or event. Analyze and contrast the voice in these selections.

Reading beyond the encyclopedia and history textbooks will give students deep levels of background and character information, enabling them to write with voice. Ask students to imagine what it would have been like to live in a particular time and place. For example, wide reading might enable them to imagine that they are one of the soldiers on the ground in Pickett's Charge or a nurse who was on site after the battle, and they can write about the event with voice. Use mentor text such as *Smoky Mountain Rose: An Appalachian Cinderella* by Alan Schroeder to model how students can create voice that reflects a specific culture. Tell the same folktale using voices from different cultures.

Questions to Use When Conferring about Voice

Foster a student's use of voice in individual pieces during conferencing. Ask *who*, *what*, *when*, *where*, and *why* questions that are specific to the piece to help the writer bring the piece to life. Here are some general questions that can be used when conferring to bring out the student's voice:

- How can you write this piece so that it speaks to the reader?

- What details can you add to help the reader share your strong feelings?

- How can you revise this section so the reader feels …?

- Can you use punctuation, such as quotation marks or exclamation points, to show your feelings?

- Let's think of some ways to put your personal slant (point of view, attitude, or perspective) on this piece.

- Can you put in special sound effects such as *Splat!* and *Grrrrr!?*

- How can you make this piece sound fresh and not trite?

- What will happen to this piece if you make your characters talk?

- How can you make this piece tug at the readers' heartstrings?

- How can you make this piece stimulate the readers' brain?

- Can you revise this section using a clearer voice to make it easier for the reader to follow? Where might the reader be confused?

- What is your role as a writer (observer and advertiser)?

- To whom are you writing this piece? (self, public, best friend, grandmother, U.S. senator, etc.)

- What might be another format you can use to convey your voice? (speech, news article, letter)

Tips for Bringing Out the Student's Voice

Follow these tips to help you bring out your students' voices:

➤ Explore voice using literature throughout the year.

➤ Share literature with the class where the author's voice is strong.

➤ Remember that classic, informational, or argumentative writing are often good models for voice.

➤ Share student selections that demonstrate effective writing with voice.

➤ Provide opportunities for topic choice in student writing.

➤ Embrace other ways of speaking, such as out-of-school voices or voices from different cultures.

- Try to influence your students' voices in positive ways without silencing them.

- Describe voice as the writer's desire to speak in a certain way to the reader or to put his or her personal slant on a piece.

- Talk to students about the author's voice in narrative, informative, and argumentative literature.

- Contrast short pieces with strong voice (e.g., an episode from a biography) with pieces on the same topic or event that have weaker voice (e.g., report on the same event from an encyclopedia or textbook).

- Discuss with students when and why they use different voices in different contexts.

- In light of technology, talk with students about how bringing other authors' voices into their writing compares with plagiarism.

Sentence Fluency

"Sentence fluency is the auditory trait. We read for it with our ears as much as with our eyes. As we take in the words and phrases on the page, ideally, we hear a melody."

—Ruth Culham (2003, 176)

When sentences flow without hesitation, like a smooth current of a river, the melodic cadence longs to be read aloud. The words, phrases, and sentences have rhythm, power, and movement. The real test of sentence fluency is how it sounds when read aloud. Read these excerpts aloud from a few of our favorite mentor texts and listen to the patterns, lengths, and styles of the sentences. This rhythmic and graceful language exemplifies the trait of sentence fluency.

"Far, far out to sea, land is only a memory, and empty sky touches the water. Just beneath the surface is a tangle of weed and driftwood where tiny creatures cling. This is the nursery of a sea turtle."

(*One Tiny Turtle* by Davies and Chapman, 6–7).

"Dusk is the name for evening twilight. Dusk gives the signal for night to be born. Dusk deepens the colors of ordinary things. Even the common grass takes on a luster that makes you stop to look. In the summer, dusk hisses on the sprinklers. It flushes out millions of mosquitoes and armies of bats to eat them. Fireflies appear, swimming through the air, writing bright messages in secret code. Slowly dusk pours the syrup of darkness into the forest."

(*Twilight Comes Twice* by Ralph Fletcher, 7–9)

"A day or so later, John Henry saw a crew building a road. At least, that's what they were doing until they came on a boulder right smack-dab where the road was supposed to go. This was no ordinary boulder. It was as hard as anger and so big around, it took half a week for a tall man to walk from one side to the other."

(*John Henry* by Julius Lester, 9)

How to Teach Sentence Fluency

When teaching sentence fluency, focus on helping students listen to the rhythm and flow in literature and in their own writing. Students learn to identify the "hiccups" in the passage where they begin to think, "That just doesn't sound right." They learn to listen for easy-flowing text that makes the reader think, "I like the way that sounds." Mem Fox (1993) reminds us that frequently reading aloud is perhaps the best means to develop a sense of rhythm and fluency in writing. Students of any age like to be read to. Read aloud with expression to help students develop an ear for how sentence fluency can enhance the meaning of the author's message. Read aloud to hear fluency; how sentence length and variety fit together like pieces of a puzzle, figurative language sings a melody, and the effortless flow of the passage brings meaning and joy to the reader.

Writers, while learning to structure a sentence, benefit tremendously by hearing multiple samples from read-alouds, picture books, prose, and poetry. Without exposure, their writing may reflect the simple language patterns encountered in the text they use to develop their reading skills. As readers develop, include activities that give students opportunities to read with expression and fluency, such as readers theater, choral reading, echo reading, and even poetry recitals. Remember, both you and your students need time to rehearse before reading aloud and performing in order to demonstrate the natural rhythm of sentence fluency.

Much of sentence fluency relies on sentence structure, length, and variety. As we teach our youngest writers, our focus lies in the development and appearance of a simple sentence and then of multiple sentences. These simple sentences are celebratory beginnings, but we soon guide students away from these short, choppy statements, combining them into more complex sentences. As students develop as writers, our instruction of sentence structure should progress in a manner similar to Figure 6.10.

Figure 6.10 Sentence Fluency Pyramid

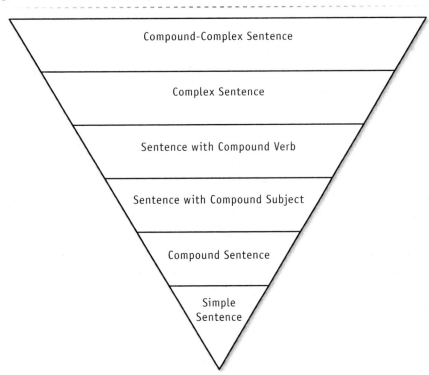

The length of sentences naturally develops through writing with different sentence structure. Developing longer and more complex sentences fascinates some early writers. They often use too many sentences with similar sentence structure which become mundane and repetitive for the reader. Teach students how sprinkling in a few short sentences that grab the reader's attention, emphasize change, or stress a point can improve the rhythm and flow of their writing.

Along with sentence types and lengths, writing seems to blossom when students are taught that constructing sentences with variety can improve the meaning and add interest for their readers. Teaching with young writers includes using different types of sentences, varying the beginning of sentences, and using fragments. Writing is communicating, and just like conversations, writing should reflect the author's feelings and intonations. Ask questions, convey information, use commands and requests, and express thoughts in daily conversations. When students make the connection between our natural language and writing, they begin to understand the purpose of the four fundamental sentence types.

- Declarative sentences provide information and/or ideas.

- Interrogative sentences interrogate, or ask questions.

- Exclamatory sentences express the writer's strong emotions.

- Imperative sentences express a command or make a request. They are often confused with sentence fragments. They have an implied subject, "you." (e.g., (You) take me to the party.)

The challenge is not to teach students to recognize the four sentence types but to use them effectively in their writing. Be cautious of asking writers to write a paragraph and include three or four types of sentences. Depending on the topic and purpose of the writing, using that many different types may result in awkward and unnatural written language. Because most writing consists of declarative sentences, teach students to use interrogative, exclamatory, and imperative sentences to surprise the reader, give emphasis to an idea, or create a rhythmic flow to their writing. Teach students that using the four sentence types automatically creates more interesting writing.

Varying sentence beginnings has much to do with using transition words and phrases to link a writer's thoughts together. Even kindergarten and first-grade students begin using simple transitions such as *first*, *next*, *then*, and *finally*. Provide lists of transition words to support student writing, but only after modeling lessons and noting students' understanding of the concept. We introduce several options for beginning sentences, based on the developmental level and interest of students, such as:

- **An adjective:** White and fluffy, the kitten...

- **Adverbs, clauses, and phrases:** Slowly, the fox crept toward... Moving quickly toward the prey,...

- **A prepositional phrase:** Before the game,...

- **A gerund:** a verb acting as a noun (Living alone,...)

- **An infinitive phrase:** To + verb (To avoid a sunburn,...)

- **An interjection:** Oh! There you are! or Mmmm, this is delicious!

Teach fragments as a way to develop a strong understanding of sentence structure and types. It is true that most state writing assessment scoring engines and most English teachers everywhere do not approve of the use of sentence fragments. Teach students the difference between formal writing and the craft of writing like an author. Look closely at some of our most beloved authors. Notice they challenged the rules of written language and took risks. They use fragments to create stellar models of rhythm and prose. We cannot simply ignore fragments when exploring sentence lengths in *Bedhead* by Margie Palatini (2003) or dialogue in *The Music of Dolphins* by Karen Hesse (1998). So, discuss how and why the author used sentence fragments and the difference in the style and energy they make in the sentence fluency of the text. These texts and others provide a model as students are guided to play with reorganizing sentences and adding phrases to create passages readers will enjoy.

This opening excerpt from *Slam!* by Walter Dean Myers (1998) demonstrates many elements of sentence structure, length, and variety.

"Basketball is my thing. I can hoop. Case closed. I'm six four and I got the moves, the eye, and the heart. You can take my game to the bank and wait for interest. With me it's not like playing a game, it's like the only time I'm being for real. Bringing the ball down the court makes me feel like a bird that just learned to fly. I see my guys moving down in front of me and everything feels and looks right. Patterns come up and a small buzz comes into my head that starts to build up and I know it won't end until the ball swishes through the net."

—Walkter Dean Myers (1996, 1)

Types of Lessons to Teach Sentence Fluency

Sentence fluency lessons help students develop an understanding of sentence structure, sentence variety, and the flow of language. As with word choice, have fun with sentence fluency and create games and chants that engage students in sentence development. Encourage students to take a risk and try sentence patterns that create energy and interest.

Practice creating sentences orally with young writers to develop an understanding of sentence parts. For example, provide students with a subject such as *All six children…*, and ask groups of students to come up with the predicate. Share responses, stating the entire sentence. Later, provide labels *subject* and *predicate* for students to hold and each identify the part. Increase difficulty by adding a prepositional phrase or other parts of speech. Students will enjoy working in groups, using individual whiteboards to record responses. Increase the level of difficulty by giving the predicate, or not revealing what it is that they must then label and record their response (e.g., Provide: *took a bath;* Student response is subject: *My dirty brother*). Teach students to use questioning to expand their sentence by adding details. Ask *who, what, where, when, why,* and *how.* Students enjoy using *Writing Detectives* and *High Five Sentences* to develop their sentences, as seen in Figures 6.11 and 6.12.

Figure 6.11 Elements to Construct Sentences Sample 1

Writing Detective Sentence Cards

Teacher Directions: Cut out the cards below on the dotted lines and distribute them to students to help create sentences.

Be a Writing Detective!	Be a Writing Detective!
Who?	Who?
What?	What?
When?	When?
Where?	Where?
Why?	Why?

(Gentry, McNeel, and Wallace-Nesler 2012 b–c)

Figure 6.12 Elements to Construct Sentences Sample 2

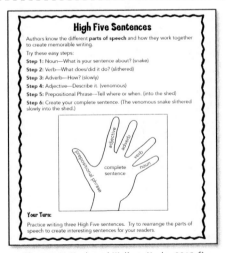

High Five Sentences

Authors know the different **parts of speech** and how they work together to create memorable writing.

Try these easy steps:

Step 1: Noun—What is your sentence about? (snake)

Step 2: Verb—What does/did it do? (slithered)

Step 3: Adverb—How? (slowly)

Step 4: Adjective—Describe it. (venomous)

Step 5: Prepositional Phrase—Tell where or when. (into the shed)

Step 6: Create your complete sentence. (The venomous snake slithered slowly into the shed.)

Your Turn:

Practice writing three High Five sentences. Try to rearrange the parts of speech to create interesting sentences for your readers.

(Gentry, McNeel, and Wallace-Nesler 2012 f)

Invite students to explore sentence structure in authentic settings. Have students work in groups to collect five to eight sentences from one media source such as a newscast, magazine article, brochure, advertisement, or recorded conversation. Then have students identify simple, compound, complex, or compound–complex sentences and discuss and note the frequency of each structure or type using a graph to record results.

Encourage students to use long and short sentences to create patterns and rhythm in their writing. Using a passage from literature, newspaper, magazine, or their own drafts, ask students to count and record the number of words in each sentence. Read the text aloud and note the pattern and flow of the written text. Do the sentence lengths enhance or hinder the fluency of the passage? Revise the text by combining sentences or adding shorter sentences for emphasis. In *The Long and Short of It* (Figure 6.13), students count words and use highlighters to identify sentence length.

Figure 6.13 Creating Patterns of Rhythm Sample

(Gentry, McNeel, and Wallace-Nesler 2013 g)

Demonstrate lessons that show writers using a variety of ways to begin sentences. After modeling, have students circle or highlight the first word in each sentence of a provided text or their own draft. Initially, focus on the sameness of the first word, and use transition words to link sentences together. In Figure 6.14, the focus turns to using different parts of speech to add variety to the beginning of sentences as demonstrated in *Sentence Switcharoo*.

Figure 6.14 Varying Sentence Structure Sample

Sentence Switcharoo

Authors change the beginning of sentences to avoid repetition and provide variety and interest for their readers.

Use a picture and learn to Sentence Switcharoo.

Adjectives	Nouns	Verbs	Prepositional Phrases
cute	raccoons	climbing	on a gnarly tree branch
cuddly	critters	searching	above the ground
mischievous	creatures	scrambling	in a huge oak tree
three	mammals	playing	beside the tree
	bandits	watching	

Sentence #1:
Three cute, cuddly critters were playing in a huge oak tree.

Sentence #2:
Playing in a huge oak tree were three cute, cuddly critters.

Sentence #3:
In a huge oak tree, three cute, cuddly critters were playing.

Your Turn:
Select a picture. Create a chart like the one shown above. Write as many words as you can in each column. Circle one or more ideas in each column. Create three sentences that begin with different words or phrases.

(Gentry, McNeel, and Wallace-Nesler 2012 f)

Use the following strategies to teach students how to improve fluency in their writing:

- **Use literature** to show students how punctuation plays an important part in the movement of the text and can completely change the meaning for a reader. Demonstrate the lingering effect of an ellipsis, how commas separate an appositive to provide more specific information, and how semicolons add phrasing, meaning, and flow to their writing. Students enjoy how Lynne Truss uses punctuation to play with sentence meaning in her books *Twenty-Odd Ducks: Why, Every Punctuation Mark Counts!* and *Eats, Shoots, and Leaves: Why Commas Really Do Make a Difference!*

- **Listen to recordings of audiobooks** or authors reading their books and poetry. Many are available for free on the Internet. Students are fascinated to hear the actual author sharing his or her text.

- Teach students to **read their writing aloud** with tone and expression, to a partner, or into a whisper phone to check for sentence fluency. Use questions such as *Is it easy to read?, Does it have expression?,* and *What might make it sound even better?* (A whisper phone is a simple device that is usually made from plastic piping. Students can use the phone to quietly read aloud, and the sound is funneled directly back to students' ears.)

- **Listen to audio recordings** of musical lyrics, poetry, advertisements, commercial jingles, raps, rhymes, podcasts, and speeches. These are fun and interesting resources for exploring sentence fluency. Dr. Martin Luther King, Jr.'s speech, "Letter from Birmingham Jail," is an exemplary choice for the use of sentence fluency to enhance meaning.

Questions to Use When Conferring about Sentence Fluency

The art of understanding and writing with sentence fluency takes years of exposure to quality texts and hours of practice. Praise sentence correctness and use words to connect sentences and paragraphs. Celebrate attempts at patterns, rhythm, and flow found in student writing. Use the following guiding questions to further develop sentence fluency:

- Do the sentences flow from one to another when you read them aloud?

- Can you read your writing with expression?

- Are your sentences complete and correct?

- How can we combine short, choppy sentences to help your writing become easier to read?

- How can we create shorter sentences from this rather lengthy sentence?

- Where have you included different sentence types?

- How can we vary the beginning of your sentences?

- What transition word or phrase might you use to move the reader from one sentence or paragraph to the next?

- How can you use punctuation to add interest and spark for the reader?

- Let's read your writing/this section aloud and listen to the pattern of the sentences. Did you enjoy reading the passage?

Suggestions for Teaching Sentence Fluency

When conferring and assessing, check not only for sentence structure in students' writing but also look beyond the actual text. This is not easy. Our natural instinct is to read the writing, searching for spelling, punctuation, and whether the sentences are structured correctly. Take the time to read it aloud, mentally editing convention errors along the way, and listen to the pulse and flow of what the young writer wants to express. Sentence fluency is known as the auditory trait most effectively taught through exploring the rich, interesting language of favorite authors. Following is an additional list of a few mentor texts that can be used when teaching sentence fluency.

All the Places to Love by Patricia MacLachlan

Bat Loves the Night by Nicola Davies

Brave Irene by William Steig

Bridge to Terabethia by Katherine Paterson

Dogteam by Gary Paulsen

Dream Weaver by Jonathan London

Fly Away Home and *Whales Passing* by Eve Bunting

Follow the Drinking Gourd by Jeanette Winter

Joyful Noise: Poems for Two Voices by Paul Fleischman

Owl Moon by Jane Yolen

Rosa by Nikki Giovanni

Sadako and the Thousand Paper Cranes by Eleanor Coerr

Stellaluna and *Verdi* and *Crickwing* by Janell Cannon

Stopping by Woods on a Snowy Evening by Robert Frost and Susan Jeffers

Thank You, Mr. Falker by Patricia Polacco

The Magic Hat by Mem Fox

The Table Where Rich People Sit by Byrd Baylor

Where the Sidewalk Ends and *Falling Up* by Shel Silverstein

Word Choice

It is the purposeful selection and use of effective words and phrases that create the inviting settings, memorable characters, realistic action, and heightened emotions that is known as the trait of word choice. Writers are careful to select the right word at the right time, using precise language that clarifies the message for their reader. Although using exceptional and interesting vocabulary can enhance a writer's word choice, having the ability to use everyday language correctly and naturally can prove to be just as effective.

The purpose, audience, and voice of the writing often influences the writer's choice of words. Narrative writing showcases word choice and brings the reader or listener into the story with imagery that evokes a mental picture. The "show, don't tell" approach uses descriptive, sensory words that clarify and expand the story's ideas. The use of strong word choice can sway the reader to consider alternative viewpoints in persuasive writing. In informational writing, the writer selects specific and accurate vocabulary to explain and inform while always being sensitive to the audience. Strong word choice enhances and expands each of these writing genres while figurative language, such as alliteration, simile, and metaphor, is used effectively to enrich the writing.

How to Teach Word Choice

Understanding the importance of strong word choice not only plays a valuable role in writing but also communicates ideas and thoughts orally. Teaching should encourage students to be risk takers who carefully consider strong and relevant words that capture the thoughts and feelings in their writing and speaking. It is no secret that students with larger vocabularies are certainly at an advantage when focusing on the trait of word choice. Young students exposed to purposeful conversation and quality literature may use interesting, descriptive language in their speech before it appears in their writing. They may fear using words incorrectly in their writing, or they may be unsure of the "right way" to spell the word, often settling for a simpler word. However, with encouragement and support, students soon begin trying out new words and phrases in their writing. It will take many attempts and misuse of words before students fully understand the meaning of word choice.

The number of students that enter school with a deficit in vocabulary development is staggering. Although the trait of word choice is more than just vocabulary, as a student's vocabulary develops, the number of interesting, descriptive words available for writing also increases. Exposure to new words in oral conversation and quality literature can support and enhance a student's developing vocabulary as well. Not only should we teach and encourage parents to hold meaningful conversations with their children, but we also need to hold these same conversations with our students. Asking questions, expanding their thoughts, and restating their ideas exposes students to new vocabulary. When teaching and reading text, think aloud throughout the process, using vocabulary that will expand your students' word choices.

Worried they may not understand? It's simple. When using an unfamiliar word, give a two- or three- word definition. Here's an example from *Stellaluna* by Janell Cannon, "Each night, Mother Bat would carry Stellaluna clutched [held tightly] to her breast as she flew out to search for food" (1993, 2).

As with other traits, but even more so with the trait of word choice, reading quality literature—narrative, persuasive, informative, and poetry—exposes students to the author's craft. With support and guidance, they soon develop an "I can write like that" attitude and begin using interesting words and phrases. Teaching word choice enables even the most reluctant writers to take an average piece of writing and revise it, using vivid, descriptive vocabulary; strong verbs; specific nouns and adjectives; and figurative language to express their thoughts and enhance the message for the reader.

Teach students the importance of using descriptive words to create images, that showing is so much better than telling, and when we write through the senses our readers join us in our writing journey. Begin this process by showing students how readers depend on the author's writing, their own prior knowledge, and background experiences to construct mental images as they read.

As visualization is taught to build comprehension in reading and other content areas, it is important to share the connection to writing. For example, Roald Dahl uses descriptive and precise word choice to create not only a visual image for his readers but to also stir the senses.

In this selection from *The Twits* (1998), his description of Mr. Twit's eating habits not only creates a mental image, but we can smell the aroma of the tangled heap of facial hair. Dahl does not just "tell" the reader that Mr. Twit is a messy eater. Instead, he "shows" the reader and paints a picture with word choice that is both exciting and memorable.

"...there were always hundreds of bits of old breakfasts and lunches and suppers sticking to the hairs around his face. They weren't big bits, mind you, because he used to wipe those off with the back of his hand or on his sleeve while he was eating. But if you looked closely (not that you'd ever want to) you would see tiny little specks of dried-up scrambled eggs stuck to the hairs, and spinach and tomato ketchup and fishsticks and minced chicken livers and all the other disgusting things Mr. Twit liked to eat.

If you looked closer still (hold your noses, ladies and gentlemen), if you peered deep into the moustachy bristles sticking out over his upper lip, you would probably see much larger objects that had escaped the wipe of his hand, things that had been there for months and months, like a piece of maggoty green cheese or a moldy old cornflake or even the slimy tail of a tinned sardine."

—Roald Dahl (1998, 6–7)

Read the descriptive texts with students without sharing illustrations. Then, share the mental image created through thinking aloud and have students draw a visual representation of the passage. Talk about and highlight sensory language in the text the author used to support their illustrations. Once this is modeled, provide additional texts with descriptive characters, actions, or settings and invite students to identify key words that help them as they create their own visual images. When they share, their representations will have similarities created from the author's word choice and differences that represent their schema and background experiences.

Poetry is another resource to show students how to use their senses to create word pictures for readers. Poems like "I Wish I Had a Dragon" and "My Neighbor's Dog Is Purple" by Jack Prelutsky or "Dragonfly" by Georgia Heard and texts such as *The Salamander Room* by Anne Mazer, *A Quiet Place* by Douglas Wood, *Greyling* and *Owl Moon* by Jane Yolen, and *Fireflies* by Julie Brinckloe represent a few texts shared with students to develop descriptive language and explore the use of sensory words.

Teach students that writers know the importance of selecting words that are colorful and precise, yet accurate. Strong, active verbs give the reader the exact image the author wishes to portray.

Use a simple sentence like *The girl went out the back door.* By substituting a strong verb, the sentence takes on a whole different meaning, for example:

The girl stomped out the back door.

The girl bounced out the back door.

The girl sprinted out the back door.

The girl tiptoed out the back door.

Support students in selecting active verbs for their writing by creating wall charts filled with vivid verbs collected from favorite literature like *Brave Irene* and *Sylvester and the Magic Pebble* by William Steig. Picture books by Janell Cannon like *Stellaluna* and *Crickwing* are full of strong verbs like *crooned, clutched, swooped, ached, scrambles, stammered, gasped, chortled, clobbered,* and *toil.* Even the youngest writers create action verbs with displayed charts entitled, *I can …* (giggle, smile, swim, or whisper) or *Animals can . . .* (trot, wag, pant, or meow) which are lists of words they are familiar with or find in their texts throughout the year.

When teaching about using precise words in writing, don't just focus on verbs, but also include the use of specific nouns and adjectives in writing. The main idea is to teach students to select words that help the reader envision the story, setting, and characters exactly the way they want. Select a sentence from a student's writing, with permission, or create a sentence to model like *The table was set with meat, potatoes, vegetables, and dessert for dinner.* Have students close their eyes and imagine what is on the table, and then have them quickly jot down their thoughts. While creating a chart, share and record responses. Imagine the variety of dinner items listed on the chart. Adding precise nouns and adjectives removes the guessing game and brings both the reader and writer together on the same page *Grandmother's china waited to be filled with roasted turkey, creamy mashed potatoes and gravy, my mom's famous corn soufflé, and pumpkin pie, as we gathered at the table.* Again, even the youngest writers can learn to write with more specific word choice by using a simpler statement. For example, *I see a ball.* Ask, "What kind of ball? Basketball? Baseball? Rubber ball? Or *The dog is cute.* Ask questions for clarification like, "What kind of dog? Poodle? Boxer? Chihuahua? Dachshund? What makes the dog cute? Wagging tail? Spots? With guiding questions, one kindergarten student revised and wrote: *My pdl hs krle lks* (My poodle has curly locks).

Teach students to use available resources like word charts on the walls, personal word walls, and of course the thesaurus. Anchor word charts and personal word walls/dictionaries are typically full of words that are familiar and comfortable. Build on this vocabulary through word choice mini-lessons. A thesaurus is an author's friend, but it can be a student's worst nightmare when their writing becomes "thesaurus overload!" You know what we are talking about. The student who gets a list of synonyms and replaces common words with longer, fancier synonyms regardless of the meaning or connotation. A second grader, Braden, finding synonyms from word charts, revised his family story to include *I think my mom is really ancient because she has white hair* and *My little sister is rotund!* Hopefully, his parents had a good chuckle at open house while reading this memorable story. When teaching young students about synonyms and using a thesaurus, it is important to emphasize the semantic meaning and degrees of a word, as well as understanding connotations (e.g., chubby vs. rotund). Students should recognize that common words have a place in literature and our writing, and that "fancier" is not always better.

Another key area to address when teaching word choice is figurative language. Figurative language is commonplace in everyday conversations when making comparisons or bringing drama and emphasis to a topic. Whether present in speech or writing, the listener or reader must interpret and "figure out" the meaning related to the figure of speech. Authors use these words and phrases to create interest and precise images and to entertain. Ralph Fletcher states, "It's up to us to create conditions where students will want to play with language" (2010, 80). We use literature, music, poetry, newspapers, magazines, TV, and print ads to teach and interpret words and phrases used in figurative language. Students enjoy exploring and learning about figurative language. It should be a natural, not forced, addition that adds dimension and interest to their writing.

Examples of figures of speech we commonly address when teaching writers are:

- **Alliteration:** a poetic device that involves the repetition of initial consonant sounds of several words (e.g., *The pot of purple pansies plopped off the porch rail*)

- **Hyperbole:** a word phrase used by speakers and writers for emphasis or effect (e.g., *She cried a river*)

- **Idiom:** a word phrase that implies something other than the literal meaning of the individual words (e.g., *sick as a dog*, *costs an arm and a leg*, and *break a leg*)

- **Metaphor:** a comparison of two unlike objects or ideas without the use of the words *like* or *as* (e.g., *The test was a walk in the park*)

- **Simile:** a comparison of two things using the words *like* or *as* (e.g., *hair like silk*, *as happy as a witch in a broom factory*, and *slow as molasses*)

- **Personification:** the use of words to give human characteristics to objects (e.g., *The moon smiled in the midnight sky*)

- **Onomatopoeia:** a word or group of words that imitate sounds (e.g, *with a click of the mouse*, *the buzzing in my ear*, and *her chattering teeth*)

During a mini-lesson on similes, first-grader Sophia announced, "My mom says I'm as cute as a button, but I think buttons are kind of ugly. Don't you?" When his class used digital cameras to take pictures for a book on friendship, English language learner Alan sprinted out the door when he heard his teacher state, "Everyone be careful when you snap the pictures, you might chop off your friend's head!" It is important to remember that young students and English language learners often take figures of speech literally. Students must be taught that some figures of speech do not mean what they say. Help them clarify the meaning and understand the author's purpose for word choice.

Types of Lessons to Teach Word Choice

Model and teach students to "read like a writer." During read-alouds, select a few words and phrases and discuss the meaning of the author's word choice. Ask questions about why authors selected a specific word or phrase. For example, in *Chrysanthemum* by Kevin Henkes (2008), the other students make fun of the character's name, and he writes: "Chrysanthemum wilted." Why not use cried or frowned? Showing students techniques from the text sparks interest and provides choices they may use in their own writing.

Create an environment where students talk about words and engage in finding, sharing, and celebrating words and phrases. Teach mini-lessons to encourage students to be on the lookout for words in all subject areas, TV, conversations, and announcements. We display charts with titles such as *Awesome Adjectives*, *Vivid Verbs*, and *Check Out This Word*. Students write their words on sticky notes and add them to the charts. Opportunities for sharing and discussing are valued and exciting as students add favorites to their personal dictionaries and/or notebooks. Students become word collectors and have folder and notebook pages of "Words I Love" with words that are fun to say, silly to hear, or just plain interesting, like *precious* and *opulent*.

Teach students to be observers of their surroundings. Take a nature walk, visit another classroom, tour the principal's office, or simply sit quietly for a few minutes and observe. Give students two to three minutes to record everything they observed. Now go through the list and note to which sense it is related (e.g., messy desk—sight). Have students create five columns and add one of the five senses as the heading for each column. Next, give students a few more minutes to record their observations under each column. The idea here is to help students understand that authors use more than their sight to help us "see" the story. To bring the reader into the writing, an author depends on sensory language. To help students develop their descriptive writing, try the mini-lessons in Figure 6.15 and 6.16.

Figure 6.15 Five Senses Activity 1

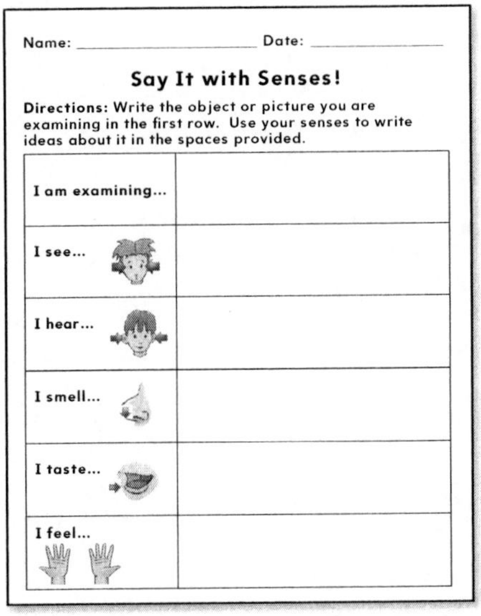

Name: ____________________ Date: ______________

Say It with Senses!

Directions: Write the object or picture you are examining in the first row. Use your senses to write ideas about it in the spaces provided.

I am examining...	
I see...	
I hear...	
I smell...	
I taste...	
I feel...	

(Gentry, McNeel, and Wallace-Nesler 2013 b)

Figure 6.16 Five Senses Activity 2

Focusing on the Five Senses

Authors use **sensory details** to make words, pictures, and stories come alive in their readers' minds, which helps them understand and enjoy the story even more.

Sight: blurred, freckled, glittering, radiant, smudged, tarnished	
Smell: aromatic, fruity, musty, pungent, rancid, spicy, smoky	
Sound: crackle, melodic, murmur, rhythmic, rustle, whimper	
Taste: delectable, delish, nauseating, scrumptious, tart, tangy	
Touch: bristly, chilly, gritty, prickly, slimy, slushy, velvety, wet	

Your Turn:

Use a Five Senses Web to generate words that paint pictures in your readers' minds. Collect sensory words to add to your notebook and use in your writing.

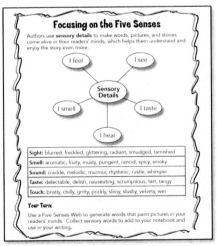

(Gentry, McNeel, and Wallace-Nesler 2012 f)

Talk to students about overused words, and create word webs or charts with alternative synonyms and antonyms they may use in their writing. We often visit classrooms where students have pages and pages of synonyms in their writing folders or notebooks. This can encourage writers to substitute one word for another without consideration of the actual meaning of the word. To develop word choice that is more natural for student writing, create a class and/or personal chart with overused words and have students add synonyms they know and understand through conversations and reading. Students learn that words are used to entertain and inform readers, not to impress them. For example:

big	little	look	walk	ran/run
enormous	teensy	peer	strut	sprinted
huge	wee	glanced	stroll	jogged

Be careful when "burying" overused words, as some students take words very literally. Mika was struggling with her writing, and her teacher sat down to conference. Noticing she had dialogue started, Mrs. Lee asked how her writing was progressing. Mika told her, "Not too good. I can't think of a word to go here." Mrs. Lee stated, "How about said?" Mika replied, "Mrs. Lee, you know we buried said."

Provide simple sentences and paragraphs sprinkled with overused, common words. Have students work with a partner to revise words and phrases to create a precise and descriptive piece of writing. Challenge them to consider active verbs, specific nouns and adjectives, and figurative language, but only when necessary. It is fun and interesting to hear the variety and creativity students use in their writing.

Figure 6.17 shows the value of using specific word choice to "show" the reader our writing. Whether talking about the color of a character's dress in a narrative or the color of a particular fish in an informational piece, writers are taught that they should choose the best word possible. If they write *blue*, we ask "Is it dark blue or light blue?" And then, "Is it aquamarine, teal, or periwinkle?" Some teachers refer to this as "hitting the target" or "using the money words," and we want students to spend their words wisely.

Figure 6.17 Sample Word-Use Activity

Be Specific!

Authors use specific words, such as proper nouns, to create a clear picture in the reader's mind.

A **common noun** is a person, place, or thing.

A **proper noun** is the specific name of a person, place, or thing and always begins with a capital letter.

Common Noun	Proper Noun	Descriptive Words
car	Ford Thunderbird	1955 candy apple red convertible
street	Washington Avenue	narrow congested

- The car raced down the street.
- The 1955 candy apple red Ford Thunderbird convertible raced down narrow, congested Washington Avenue.

Your Turn:

Writers, be specific using these words. Then, create and add new sentences to your notebook. Remember to capitalize the proper nouns.

Common Noun	Proper Noun	Descriptive Words
hamburger		
store		
teacher		
band		
dog		

(Gentry, McNeel, and Wallace-Nesler 2012 f)

Engage students in the word play of figurative language. Identify and collect words and phrases from a variety of genres. Acknowledge and celebrate when students begin including figurative language in their own writing. Even when they are confused about meaning, remember they are making attempts. Guide students to understanding and share alternatives and options to support them in using figures of speech effectively. In Figure 6.18, students illustrate four figures of speech, and partners try to guess the word, phrase, or sentences the pictures represent. Teachers can select one to use with younger students.

Fig. 6.18 Sample Figures of Speech Chart

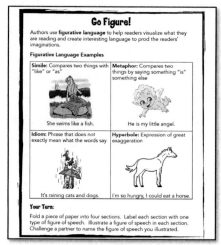

(Gentry, McNeel, and Wallace-Nesler 2012 f)

Questions to Use When Conferring about Word Choice

Asking students a few simple questions can stimulate thinking about word choice as well as clarify their selection when words and phrases are used incorrectly. As students develop an understanding of word choice, questioning and guiding students to alternatives is much more effective than merely pointing out their mistakes. This list is a sampling of questions to ask students.

- Who is your audience for this piece of writing?

- Are you writing to inform or entertain?

- Are there words that repeat too often?

- Are there words that do not seem to fit?

- How might you use your senses to add details that clarify the meaning of your writing?

- Which are your favorite words or phrases in this piece?

- Which verbs are active and describe what is happening?

- What phrase or figure of speech might help the reader understand your thinking?

- Is your choice of words precise and specific?

- What might be another word for...?

- Did you use words and phrases to create vivid images that will linger in the minds of your reader?

- Are there words or phrases that might be unknown to your reader, like jargon, localisms, clichés, and acronyms?

Suggestions for Teaching Word Choice

Keep a word journal and encourage students to be word collectors. Use small notebooks or electronic notepads and jot down interesting words, phrases, and quotes heard in everyday conversations and media, or read on the Internet, signs, posters, or newspapers. Students begin to value words and phrases of loved ones, like Grandpa's favorite saying or the English neighbor's word for *elevator*. Keeping note of words that are overused, vague, and annoying can help us with writing. You may wish to make a word collage in your classroom and have students add the good and the not so good.

Teach students to love the dictionary and like the thesaurus. We want students to avoid getting hung up on "just the right" word when drafting and writing a known word as a filler. Then they ask themselves, "What's another way to say that?" This helps students write with less restraint and more fluency. Ask students to use the dictionary first to help them become aware of the actual meaning of the word, find synonyms, and consider how the word may be used. Using a thesaurus may be quicker, especially when using the computer, but it does not always have the best result nor does it allow students to learn the meaning of new words.

Enjoy and have fun exploring and teaching word choice to students. It is an extraordinary feeling when students' curiosity about words unfolds, and they begin trying new and interesting words and phrases in their writing.

Conventions

"Too much correction or correction at the wrong time can be confusing, not enlightening. Remember, what you pay attention to, you reinforce."

—Donald Graves (as cited in Walshe 1981, 10)

Pay attention to conventions, which includes the use of correct capitalization, grammar usage, punctuation, and spelling that makes writing consistent and easy to read. However, many of us have memories of the teacher who gave way too much attention to conventions, returning papers that may have had brilliant content but were dripping in red ink from every page. In our workshops on conferencing with writers and scoring writing, it is most likely that when we ask teachers what they notice about the writing at first glance, we hear comments like, "The spelling is atrocious"; "I have gone over ending with punctuation a million times"; and "They know proper nouns begin with a capital." Ask yourself, why do we tend to zero right in on conventions? For the most part, we are familiar and comfortable with the writing trait of conventions. There are convention rules that are easily identified as being right or wrong, making conventions an easy first target. As teachers of writing, remember that conventions is only one of the quality traits of writing, and it typically is attended to after revising work during the editing process. Generally, teachers should pay attention to meaning and content first, then conventions. Suppose a kindergartner writes a wonderful story in invented spelling with many mechanical mistakes. Graves had the perspective that it would be prudent to choose only a few mistakes to work with.

Conventions should be taught, but mastering conventions takes time. Students need the time and opportunity to develop an "automaticity" in their early writing before focusing their attentions on conventions. This automaticity is developed through providing daily opportunities for draft writing, allowing for phonetic spelling, and developing ideas, organization, and vocabulary. According to the Common Core State Standards (2010), the grade-by-grade expectation is correct spelling of grade-level words and words that have been taught. It is important that teachers pay attention to spelling in writing and teach spelling explicitly. Students may begin going through five developmental stages of spelling beginning in kindergarten, but it may take nine years before writers spell automatically and correctly with ease.

Editing for conventions is part of a process that, along with the writer, develops in sophistication. It's not only knowledge of conventions that must develop over time; the writer must also develop consciousness for conventions and correctness. Too much attention to correctness too early may stymie the budding writer. Consider your own thoughts and feelings upon receiving the paper "dripping in red."

How to Teach Conventions

There are basically two schools of thought regarding how to address conventions. Extreme views of this dichotomy are to teach conventions through daily drill and workbook exercises or to let students write daily and learn conventions as they run into problems. If taking the first stance, instruction can be mindless and boring. If you take the second stance, you may be embracing a pipe dream and going against the research evidence for explicit and systematic teaching of basic conventions. It may be too idealistic to think that students will experiment with punctuation and solve their own problems or "catch" expert spelling by writing and reading a lot. It takes a very skillful master teacher to teach conventions and spelling solely in the context of writing while covering all the other traits of quality writing. Having students run into problems with conventions in the context of writing doesn't fix mechanics by itself. Neither extreme—teaching conventions in isolation or teaching them in context—works by itself. Conventions are best taught both explicitly and systematically in isolation and in context.

It is often no surprise when teachers like Ms. Lopez state, "I just don't get it. They're (students) doing great in grammar. I do daily fix-its, and we spend time on grammar exercises each day. Yet I'm not seeing it in their writing." When conventions are taught in insolation, students seldom transfer the skills to writing (Weaver 2008). They may have a full understanding of the rules and vocabulary but lack the ability to apply conventions to their own writing.

Consider four steps when planning for instruction of conventions in writer's workshop. First, through benchmarking, assessing, and conferencing with students, identify those deficit skills that are developmentally appropriate for students. There is no need to teach capitalization of proper nouns if the majority of students have mastered that skill. Support those students' deficits during small-group and individual conferencing sessions. Next, develop a prioritized list of mini-lessons to teach during writer's workshop. Use the editing process to share model writing and authentic student writing to identify convention errors. This list is flexible and can change based on observations of students' writing. Then, allow students time to thoroughly practice this skill during authentic writing opportunities. Students need time to experiment and make errors without judgments. Finally, expect students to be accountable for those specific skills. If you have taught, reviewed, and allowed time for practice of a convention skill, expect students to use those conventions in their writing. Create a chart entitled *Conventions We Have Learned* to remind students of the conventions they have learned and should use in their writing. Assess, teach, practice, and monitor the conventions of writing to ensure that students not only have control of their own writing conventions but are also capable of editing other text as well.

There is no doubt teaching the conventions of writing is complex. Consider the relationship of oral language with writing conventions. Imagine having a conversation and inserting *all* of the capitalization and punctuation marks that you would include in the writing of the same conversation. Conventions are not visible in oral language, but we unconsciously use voice inflections, facial expressions, and pauses when speaking. Writing, on the other hand, involves a conscious effort to correctly include capitalization, punctuation, grammar, and spelling. This contributes to the fact that capitalization is not easy for beginners nor is subject and verb agreement, especially with English language learners or students who speak nonstandard English. Punctuation includes use of periods, exclamation marks, question marks, apostrophes, ellipses, dashes, carets, quotation marks, commas, colons, parentheses, asterisks, and semicolons.

Research shows that students in the context of a vigorous writer's workshop write every day in school and run into most if not all of these punctuation marks in context by third grade (Walshe 1981). Even young writers notice authors using these marks in books that they read. Some writer's workshop advocates contend that as writers need punctuation, they often become intrigued, noticing how real writers use marks such as dashes, exclamation marks, and apostrophes and try them out in their own writing. Yet there is a big leap between running into punctuation and mastering punctuation conventions. The use of mentor texts is an extremely valuable tool for sharing conventions during writing mini-lessons. These mini-lessons provide the explicit instruction necessary to teach students the rules of conventions and encourage students to use that knowledge of conventions in their writing. As if capitalization and punctuation weren't enough, there are the often mind-boggling conventions of English spelling. Taken all at once, editing for conventions can be overwhelming.

Teaching writers how to spell is perhaps the greatest conventions challenge. Common Core State Standards (2010) state that students should know how to spell with proficiency on grade level. Yet in the past two decades, many districts have stopped teaching spelling, assigned a scaled-down list from the reading program, or replaced explicit spelling instruction with creative methods that may not be accelerating student growth. New trends, beginning in the 1990s, introduced a series of constructivist approaches, such as spelling instruction embedded in writing or delivered as "word study" (Invernizzi, Abouzeid, and Gill 1994). This latter approach encouraged students to construct their own spelling knowledge through word sorting and games via discovery method, hypothesis testing, and socialization (Wilde 1999; Bear et al. 2012). Up to this point, empirical evidence of the effectiveness of constructivist approaches has been limited (Allal 1997; Santangelo and Graham 2011; Gentry 2004; Schlagal 2002; Sharp, Sinatra, and Reynolds 2008). In practice, many of the experiments with spelling seem to have had poor results.

Teachers need a basic grade-by-grade curriculum for teaching important conventions. Once conventions are taught, they are applied and monitored in students' frequent writing. Conventions are integrated daily through modeled mini-lessons and applied during writing workshops. Correct conventions are supported in student writing with anchor charts, revisited often, and retaught in conferencing and small groups. Additionally, some complex conventions such as spelling may best be taught explicitly and systematically following a grade-by-grade curriculum or a research-based spelling book (Gentry 2004).

Types of Lessons to Teach Conventions

Lessons for conventions introduce a convention by modeling and giving students short, focused opportunities to engage in and practice using the convention in writing. Gradually release the responsibility of the use of the convention to the writer. Use anchor charts to constantly remind writers of conventions that should receive focus at a particular grade level, and use supports such as high-frequency spelling word lists attached to students' personal writing folders. In conferencing, make sure to monitor each student's use of conventions, and capitalize on teachable moments for teaching conventions in context. It is recommended that teachers allow both their observations from student writing and their curriculum guide to help them decide what conventions lessons to stress in mini-lessons. Some of our favorite conventions lessons are ones for developing awareness and good habits. The following are two great lesson ideas for conventions.

Moving to Edit

Use a multisensory, action-oriented approach to teach punctuation and capitalization beginning in first grade with a lesson called "Moving to Edit." Students up to eighth grade enjoy "Moving to Edit." Begin by teaching actions such as "karate chop" for comma and "right foot grind into the floor" for period. Model first, and then move into partner teams, triads, or quads to practice the movements. Choose a team leader to play "Simon Says" and shout out an editing mark. Figure 6.19 offers suggested actions for other common editing marks.

Figure 6.19 Movin' to Edit Actions

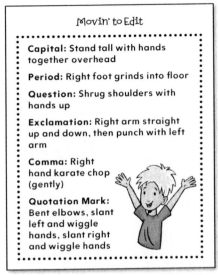

Movin' to Edit

Capital: Stand tall with hands together overhead

Period: Right foot grinds into floor

Question: Shrug shoulders with hands up

Exclamation: Right arm straight up and down, then punch with left arm

Comma: Right hand karate chop (gently)

Quotation Mark: Bent elbows, slant left and wiggle hands, slant right and wiggle hands

(Gentry, McNeel, and Wallace-Nesler 2012 b)

Students quickly learn to respond with the action as the caller shouts out "comma," "quotation mark," "exclamation," or "capital letter." Once students automatically know the movements, they enjoy editing short segments of writing shown on the board with a document camera or interactive whiteboard as the pieces are read orally at a slowed-down but expressive pace. Often, students volunteer their own pieces for group edits. In upper grades, students enjoy trying sophisticated punctuation challenges, such as, "The officer said, "Stop!" which requires seven actions, including capitalization. One fifth-grade class requested "Moving to Edit" to build awareness for the importance of editing writing samples in preparation for the state writing test. Students asked to bring their required test prep samples back to class for *Moving to Edit*. It was a great way to instill consciousness into the whole class for the importance of editing their writing samples on the state test.

Capital Rap

One of our most popular conventions lessons is "Capital Rap." It is no secret that musical rhythm, rhyme, and patterns support student learning. Using "Capital Rap" is not only fun and engaging for students but also helps them remember the rules of basic capitalization. Introduce this catchy rap, and have students snap their fingers to the beat as they review rules for capitalization. Older students enjoy creating their own beat box rhythms to accompany the verses.

Capital Rap. Capital Rap.
"I" am important.
So are you.
The beginning of a sentence is important too.
Capital Rap. Capital Rap.

(Gentry, McNeel, and Wallace-Nessler 2012b, 220)

The rap can get more sophisticated for later grades by adding verses after more sophisticated capitalization rules are taught in mini-lessons.

Capital Rap. Capital Rap.
Days of the week and
Months of the year,
Cities and states
Need capitals, it's clear!
Capital Rap. Capital Rap.

Capital Rap. Capital Rap.
Titles of a book,
Movie or TV,
A special place or holiday,
Need capitals, you see!
Capital Rap. Capital Rap.

(Gentry, McNeel, and Wallace-Nessler 2012d, 229)

Lessons such as "Moving to Edit" and "Capital Rap" bring fun and energy into the teaching of conventions, which students too often think of as boring or drudgery.

Digging into Editing

Writers are more inspired to edit when they feel like "grown-up writers," so teach them to use professional editing symbols used by real authors. By third or fourth grade, teach a lesson called "Digging into Editing" in which student-authors are encouraged to "scoop out errors to develop a clear message for their readers." First, introduce editing symbols gradually as we "teacher-edit" pieces that have already been "student-edited." Once students have been exposed to the editing symbols through our teacher-editing, introduce "Digging into Editing," and invite students to share in a group-edit as you model the use of editing marks for capitalizing, changing letters to lower case, inserting a period, deleting something, noting a spelling error, or inserting a comma. Students love learning to use these marks when they participate in peer editing because it makes them feel like a teacher, and indeed, they are! Figure 6.20 shows a "Digging into Editing" anchor chart, which students copy and paste into their personal writing folders or writers' notebooks.

Questions to Use When Conferring about Conventions

Here is a sampling of some of the recommendations and questions we use when conferencing about conventions:

- Refer back to anchor charts or mini-lessons you have taught. Example: Remember our "Dandy Dialogue" lesson when we learned to use quotation marks to create talk on paper? Where can you use quotation marks before and after the spoken words in this section?

- I like the way you checked for correct (capitalization, spelling, punctuation, or grammar). What are you not sure of?

- What did you learn about conventions in writing this piece?

- Show me what you did to make corrections.

- Where do you need to add 's in this sentence to show possession? (Use this teachable moment to explain how the 's works.)

- How might you use punctuation to express your character's feelings?

- Do your sentences sound correct? (Refer to subject–verb agreement, verb tense, use of pronouns, run on sentences, sentence fragments, etc.)

- Did you use your best spelling and resources to spell unknown words?

- Can your reader tell when a sentence begins and when it ends?

Figure 6.20 Sample Digging into Editing Anchor Chart

Digging into Editing

Authors scoop out errors to develop a clear message for their readers.
Dig into your writing and identify errors using these editing marks.

Editing Mark	Meaning	Example
≡	Capitalize	david gobbled up the grapes.
/	Change to lower case	My mother hugged Me when I Came Home.
⊙	Insert a period	The clouds danced in the sky ⊙
sp ◯	Check spelling	I laffed at the story.
∿	Transpose words or letters	How you are?
∧	Add a word or letter	Would you please pass the pizza?
∧,	Insert a comma	I have two cats, two dogs, and a goldfish.
ℯ	Delete	Will you call call me on the phone tonight?
¶	New paragraph	… in the tree. ¶ After lunch, I spent the day…

(Gentry, McNeel, and Wallace-Nesler 2012 e)

More Tips for Conventions

➤ Respond first to content and meaning and then look at problems with conventions.

➤ Have high expectations, but do recognize that a writer's ability to take responsibility for conventions develops over time.

➤ Use peer editing to increase engagement and consciousness for correct conventions.

➤ Once a conventions lesson is taught, include it on an editing checklist for students.

➤ Use the acronym CUPS to help the student remember the major conventions to check for when editing, which include *Capitalization*, *Usage*, *Punctuation*, and *Spelling*.

➤ Use anchor charts and supports such as high-frequency spelling word lists to aid students.

➤ Resist the tendency to make negative comments about mistakes in a paper.

➤ Don't overreact to convention errors. Remember, students are less motivated when conventions become the only focus of their writing.

➤ Teach students to edit not only with their eyes but also with their ears. Reading their writing aloud or having it read by a peer often helps students identify convention errors.

➤ Make the search for conventions interactive and fun with activities such as *Moving to Edit*.

➤ Engage students by using raps and jingles that help students remember important convention rules.

➤ Most importantly, keep in mind that correcting conventions errors is *not* teaching conventions. We have found the most effective way of teaching conventions is through explicit and systematic instruction.

The +1 Writing Trait: Presentation

Don't judge a book by its cover. We have certainly heard this saying before, but as careful as we are to be unbiased when scoring student writing, appearance influences our view of the writing. One piece may have impressive ideas and organization, but all the eraser marks, scratched out words, and paper crinkles are the elements that determine first impressions. Another may be beautifully typed, with impressive charts and graphs, but it lacks true development of the topic. Because teachers were finding that appearance influenced writing scores and teachers frequently included it in conventions, presentation was added as the "+1" trait in 1997.

The Northwest Regional Education Laboratory (2005), now Education Northwest, recognized presentation as important but not as valued as the other six traits, thus used the +1 to distinguish it from the others.

Teach students that drafting is messy. When students draft, encourage them to write without restraints, but that their writing must be legible and somewhat easy to read for teachers, peers, and even themselves. Presentation should be viewed as part of publishing and should focus on:

- neatness of handwriting or appropriate font styles and sizes;

- spacing of letters, words, and paragraphs on the page, or proper spacing used in keyboard;

- how white space is used to support ease of reading or emphasize text;

- how appropriate placement and use of titles, subtitles, and captions enhance the message;

- how the use of bullets or numbers may be necessary to clarify meaning;

- the use of illustrations, photographs, charts, and tables as necessary to clarify meaning and their appropriate placement in the text;

- how the product meets the requirements and criteria; and

- the overall appearance—is the writing pleasing to the eye and appealing and interesting to the reader?

To help students develop an understanding that first impressions are important, collect writing samples and use them to show both positive and negative elements of presentation. Discuss which they would select to read and why they would make that choice. Other print media such as posters, billboards, brochures, web pages, and greeting cards are resources to explore when teaching presentation. Carefully collect and share books from a variety of genres—narrative picture and chapter books, nonfiction, and poetry—to help students recognize the elements of presentation and how they are used to enhance the meaning and provide interest for the reader. For example, one of our favorite authors for demonstrating how word placement and white space on the page influences the rhythm and flow intended by the author is Byrd Baylor, in her books, *Everybody Needs a Rock* (1985) and *The Table Where Rich People Sit* (1998).

The development of presentation has much to do with pride and expectations. When students feel pleased and satisfied with their writing, those feelings of self-confidence and pride often emerge in the presentation of their drafts and finished product. Students are more apt to be mindful of presentation when they know that they or their peers may be reading their work during sharing. Lastly, expectations can either lower or heighten the quality of presentation demonstrated in students' writing.

Final Notes on the Traits of Quality Writing

Teaching mini-lessons that focus on the traits serves as an effective model for students to learn about the qualities of excellent writing. This chapter provides a foundation to support that instruction. Teach students how to use that knowledge to further develop their skills in the writing process. The chart in Figure 6.21 shows how each of the traits might fit into the writing process. We are not recommending prewrite on Monday, draft on Tuesday, revise on Wednesday, edit on Thursday, and publish on Friday. Keep in mind that successful writers think and reflect throughout the writing process. They do not typically follow a specific plan of action but create a sequence of logical steps that work for readers. Some collect the ideas and gather a basic organization in their heads and just start writing. Many revise while drafting, and they edit along the way. Provide guidance, but allow students the flexibility to do what works best for them. If it's just not working, suggest and provide options.

Figure 6.21 The Writing Process and Writing Trait Connection

Writing Process	Traits of Quality Writing
Prewriting: Thinking about a topic, purpose of the writing, audience, and format	**Ideas:** Developing a clear topic and details that support the main idea **Organization:** Considering a logical sequence and form **Voice:** Determining the purpose and audience
Drafting: Recording initial thoughts to create the first draft	Ideas and Voice continue **Organization:** Developing ideas into parts/paragraphs Consideration of: **Sentence Fluency:** Types, lengths, variety, and flow **Word Choice:** Precise, clear, descriptive, accurate
Revising: Rereading and rethinking to improve the writing; adding, deleting, developing, and adjusting	Ideas, Organization, and Voice continue Deeper focus on Sentence Fluency and Word Choice
Editing: Reviewing and correcting	**Conventions:** Capitalization, usage and grammar, punctuation, spelling
Publishing: Completing the final copy and sharing with others	**Presentation:** Creating a final product that is enjoyable to read and pleasing to the eye

Beyond teaching the language and understanding of the traits and their role in writing, success lies the value of using the traits of writing to objectively measure a student's development and performance. Use rubrics, first to clearly communicate writing expectations and then to monitor the progress of each of the traits in your students' writing. As an instructional tool, rubrics provide criteria for student self-evaluation and peer review. Students begin to independently identify areas of strength and those that need improvement. As an assessment tool, use the rubric to score writing consistently and use the information to guide future writing instruction.

There are numerous writing rubrics available in texts and on the Internet. Some resources for writing rubrics include the Northwest Regional Educational Laboratory text, *Seeing with New Eyes* (2005), and their website. Both have writing rubrics and writing samples scored with the rubrics to support learning. Texts by Ruth Culham and Vicki Spandel also serve as valuable resources when learning to use rubrics to score your students' writing. Demonstrate and encourage students to reflect on and evaluate their own work by providing student–friendly rubrics. Provide support and opportunities for small, heterogeneous groups to discuss, question, and evaluate their writing. Each informal or formal assessment of writing is meant to inform you and your students about what is known and what needs to be improved during the next writing task.

Most importantly, provide students with samples of writing that represent the different levels of the rubric. Introduce the rubric early in the year, and fully discuss the criteria and expectations for meeting mastery. For younger students, you might look at one or two traits at a time. Through this process, let students know you will be working together, developing each of these traits in their writing throughout the year.

> "As important as the traits are, they are only a tool. In the end, the real magic comes from you—and from the students who teach you."
>
> —Vicki Spandel (2008, 283)

Reflect and Review

1. What are the traits of good writing?

2. What lessons from this chapter will you implement? Consider your students' current writing needs, make a list, and prioritize lessons.

3. What do you consider essential vocabulary (and concepts) for teaching traits of good writing? Make a list of writing-related vocabulary words you want your students to use when they talk about their writing by the end of the year.

4. What are some questions you can use in conferences to steer students toward quality writing? Write two conferring questions for each trait, and compare them with a colleague.

Chapter 7

New Directions in Writing Instruction

 We believe in the future for student writers. There has never been a better time to be a writing teacher.

Technology in the Writing Classroom

The direction of technology integration in the classroom has taken a different mindset, directed by the technology-driven lifestyles of our "new" 21st century learners. Initially, we used technology to help us become better, more interesting, and more informed teachers. Today, students use technology to become better learners as we prepare them for creating, collaborating, and communicating in an ever-changing workplace.

In the article "It's Elementary! Integrating Technology in the Primary Grades," Boni Hamilton encourages technology use in the classroom by saying, "The more (technology) tools you put in the hands of students and teachers, the more technology becomes a natural and personal expression of their thinking" (2007, 15). We recognize the importance of technology in developing interesting instruction to ignite interest and grab the attention of students. Unlimited amounts of information and resources are only a search engine away to support our teaching. The use of technology such as document cameras, projectors, interactive whiteboards, and tablets can help support efficient and productive instruction. Teachers often identify these types of technology support as their means of "integrating" technology into instruction. Technology has not truly been integrated until classrooms become less teacher-centered, recognizing students as "capable, independent technology users who can create inspiring digital masterpieces..." (Blair 2012, 10). It is then that we can move from using technology that supports writing instruction to using technology that enhances student learning.

Digital Writing

The National Writing Project, in conjunction with DeVoss, Eidman-Aadahl, and Hicks, recognize digital writing as, "compositions created with, and oftentimes for reading or viewing on, a computer or other device that is connected to the Internet" (2010, 7). Students and teachers producing digital writing do more than integrate electronic or online tools into an unchanged writing curriculum. Hicks (2011) recommends that teachers provide opportunities for students to engage in three types of digital writing: writing to share, writing to collaborate, and writing to compose multi-media projects.

Writing to Share

Students can create classroom blogs and wikis to share their writing, images, illustrations, and links to resources connected to their topics. With simple guidance and often little assistance, even the youngest writers are motivated to post, revise, record, and share writing with classmates and family, using tools like Kidblog™. Students share their informal writing on social networks like Ning©, Facebook, and Twitter® without realizing they are writing for a purpose and an audience. Our challenge then is to capture that interest and motivate students to use the same media to share their writing projects. Providing an authentic audience—whether classmates, family, or literacy publications—builds accountability, responsibility, and self-esteem as writers recognize the value of purposeful writing.

Writing to Collaborate

Using applications such as Google Docs™, students can collaborate on coauthored documents. In *Technology to Teach Literacy: A Resource for K–8 Teachers*, Anderson, Grant, and Speck (2008) recognize that collaborative writing projects prepare students for being successful in higher education and in future business and industry endeavors. Participating in effective collaborative groups develops social skills by working with a diverse group, recognizing and accepting differences. Motivation and accountability heighten as all students share their knowledge and skills to work toward a common goal.

Writing to Compose Multimedia Projects

Creating podcasts, digital stories, Prezis, photo essays, portfolios, and movies are examples of writing to compose multimedia projects. Students, independently or in collaborative groups, orchestrate the compilation of text, video, audio, still images, and/or illustrations to develop multimedia digital writing projects. The use of technology in writing instruction is inevitable if we are to reach, inspire, and motivate students in today's digital world; however, the foundational components of effective writing instruction remain the same whether we are teaching traditional writing with the support of technology or teaching digital writing.

Graves's four essential elements and digital writing are connected in the following ways:

- **Time to write:** Students need time to practice the art and process of digital writing and time to reflect on computer writing projects including project goals, progress, and accomplishments. In the same way, students need time to develop computer and digital skills. We must be mindful and accepting of approximations, giving multiple opportunities to develop digital writing skills.

- **Choice of topic:** "Topic choice, a subject the child is aware that he knows something about, is at the heart of success in writing" (Graves 1985, 5). Guide students to discover personally important topics by sharing stories and literature from a variety of genres. Exploring science, social studies, art, music, and sports has never been easier than it is in today's digital world. Student-friendly sites like KidClick, Fact Monster™, and IPL2 (Internet Public Library) make exploring and researching safe, informational, and exciting.

- **Modeling:** Teachers and students can demonstrate the development of a topic, organize writing ideas, make revisions, edit, and develop the craft of writing using computers and word processing. Projectors, document cameras, interactive whiteboards, and notepads serve as a valuable means to demonstrating writing skills for both the teacher and for students. Both may use the web to find and/or produce examples of useful writing tools such as graphic organizers, poetry frames, and author web pages to support students' demonstrations.

- **Response**: Quality feedback and responding to another's digital writing promote critical thinking and communicating skills. Teacher and peer conferences, sharing, and responding in writer's workshop are opportunities to have conversations about digital writing. Blogs and wikis, or digital forums like Moodle™ provide opportunities for quality feedback as well as foster the development of a community of developing writers who help and support one another.

Writing Is Thought on Paper and Thought on a Screen

The following quote from the National Commission on Writing report *The Neglected "R": The Need for a Writing Revolution,* captures the importance of digital writing in the information age. "In today's complex, high-technology world, the importance of writing as a fundamental organizing objective of education is no less valid or practical. Writing, properly understood, is thought on paper. Increasingly, in the information age, it is also thought on screen, a richly elaborated, logically connected amalgam of ideas, words, themes, images, and multimedia designs" (2003, 13). As writing instruction becomes more and more technology-intensive, educators must provide students with a variety of technology tools to create and publish digital writing. However, for the use of technology to be an effective teaching tool, it should be used to engage students in purposeful, authentic writing activities following the dictates of process writing. In many ways, writing on paper and writing on the screen are one and the same. What has changed is that technology provides new opportunities and innovative ways for students to become better learners and better communicators in writing.

Computer-Based Writing Assessment

The use of computers to administer and score student writing is becoming the norm rather than the exception as school districts across the country pursue more efficient, economical, and uniform options for writing assessment. This new direction raises concerns by educators striving to meet the demands of mandated writing assessment.

Many teachers and students recognize the value of using computers to practice writing with word-processing revision tools like cut, copy, and paste, and editing tools like spell check. For the first time, eighth- and twelfth grade students across the nation used laptop computers to compose their essays for the 2012 National Assessment of Education Progress (NAEP) writing assessment. NAEP felt the change from pencil-paper assessment necessary because of the predominate presence of technology in the lives of students today. Fourth-grade students piloted a computer-based writing assessment in 2012 (Fleming 2012). The assumption here is that students utilizing computers routinely in academic and home settings will perform better on computer-based assessments than on traditional pen-and-paper writing assessments.

While electronic standardized-writing assessments are seemingly becoming commonplace, they are not without controversy. Many educators state these assessments neither represent "real" writing experiences nor truly reflect their students' writing abilities. The National Council of Teachers of English (NCTE) highlighted the controversy in 2013 in a position statement:

> "Research on the assessment of student writing consistently shows that high-stakes writing tests alter the normal conditions of writing by denying students the opportunity to think, read, talk with others, address real audiences, develop ideas, and revise their emerging texts over time."
> —National Council of Teachers of English (2013)

These assessments ask students to demonstrate their writing abilities in an environment that is void of collaboration, feedback from peers, and self-reflection, which are essential components practiced in writing classrooms where they are recognized as "real" writers. Furthermore, educators agree that these assessment conditions rarely, if ever, represent writing tasks practiced in 21st-century business and industry workplaces where teamwork, collaboration, and communication are encouraged and rewarded.

In some schools, writing curriculum is changed to assure that students are prepared to take computer-based writing assessments (Cunningham and Cunningham 2010). Unfortunately, with limited time for instruction, it is at the cost of less time on meaningful writing instruction and more time on prompted writing and test taking. For example, some educators interpret educational reform to dictate that students in third through fifth grades will be required to read two or three sources of information and respond to a prompt based on these sources. Sixth through twelfth graders may be required to read three to five sources of information and respond to a prompt based on those sources. To "help" teachers, districts purchase online writing tools where students practice and revise writing, score results, and develop individual and class proficiency reports. Opinions differ on the scoring accuracy of these online writing tools. According to a study conducted by Mark Shermis, little variation in scoring was evident in essays scored by educators and "autoreaders" (Schenone 2012). According to the statement by National Council of Teachers of English on machine scoring, all stakeholders—students, parents, teachers, administrators, general public—are highly concerned about the use of automated scoring systems for writing (2013).

Reasons for concern noted by NCTE and others include:

- Computers are incapable of recognizing and rating writing elements like persuasion, irony, humor, effective repetition, voice, and fluency.

- Computers use less-sophisticated methods of scoring than do teachers (e.g., scoring vocabulary by the length or number of letters of a word; scoring idea development by counting the length and number of sentences in each paragraph).

- Computer scoring can be "gamed"; students use "machine trickery" and erroneous information without writing anything with real substance and obtain a proficient score.

- Computer scoring appears to assign higher grades to essays of longer length.

- Computer scoring becomes more of a game to beat when overused for writing practice. Students submit draft after draft, making minor revisions like adding a sentence, phrase, or paragraph to see if scores increase. This process may provide immediate feedback on that specific paper, but it adds little to the development of writing skills and misrepresents the process of real writing.

- Computer-based writing assessments often result in formula writing that meets the scoring criteria of the software rather than writing with originality, creativity, and voice.

In spite of concerns about using computers to administer and score writing, the need to meet federal and state requirements of uniform standardized assessments that can be used to determine curriculum effectiveness and student proficiency gives schools few options. Even the Common Core State Standards (CCSS) initiative will soon be implementing computerized assessments for student writing (NCTE 2013). With these mandated assessments becoming more ubiquitous, educators must resist the frantic need to teach to the writing test and instead continue to use best practices in developing effective writing instruction to support their students. Teachers who base their curriculum around "Writer's Workshop and the writing process, 6+1 Traits, and modes of writing offer the best solution for producing good writers who can write to standards assessed on state writing tests and for real-world purposes" (Higgins, Miller and Wegmann 2006, 317).

Peha recommends we "teach in accordance with 'best practice' research throughout the year and spend a small amount of time, right before testing begins, to introduce students to the particulars of the testing format" (2013, 28). He further suggests we treat assessment preparation like other genre studies, allowing a few weeks to develop test-taking skills. Some activities to support students for high-stakes writing assessment as recommended by Christy (2005), Wolf and Wolf (2002), and NCTE (2013) include:

Help students become familiar with the content and format of the test. Inform students of the testing process and scoring procedures used in your assessment system. Occasionally, simulating assessment conditions, like prompted writing on beginning, middle, and end-of-year benchmarks, will decrease testing anxiety. Provide opportunities for strategic conversation to reduce the difficult task of writing to a prompt. "Understanding how to write to prompts begins with thinking and talking about prompts. As students learn to have conversations and to engage their thinking with an external idea (e.g., an idea that originated with someone else), they learn strategies for dealing with prompts" (Angelillo 2005, 22).

Provide time for reflection. Graves tells us that "Unless we show children how to read their writing, their work will not improve" (1994, xvi). Teach students to "read like a writer," identifying strengths and weaknesses and setting goals for further development. Teachers can provide assessment criteria such as rubrics and writing samples to help students recognize writing skills that need additional practice and improvement. Students can use portfolio artifacts to reflect on their writing development throughout the year. Although feedback from peers, teachers, and audiences is encouraged, students who reflect on their own work can reread, rethink, and revise during testing.

Analyze various models. Analyze writing samples from past assessments typically available from testing administrators to build understanding of scoring criteria. Help students explore examples and non examples of writing, using the assessment rubric to build understanding and familiarity with the assessment process.

Teach "test" vocabulary. Understanding vocabulary is essential to student success on writing assessments. Expose students to essential vocabulary throughout the school year during daily writing instruction and conversations with writers. Teach students how to identify key vocabulary words that may directly affect a prompted response.

Educators need not sacrifice quality instruction to prepare students for writing assessments. However, at the heart of that instruction, remember that "test preparation is not the goal. The goal of good writing instruction is to produce good writers" (Higgins, Miller, and Wegmann 2006, 316).

From Education Reform to Handwriting, Manuscript, and Cursive

Since 2010, the Common Core State Standards reform movement focusing on rigorous skills and adopted by nearly all of the states in the United States has made writing in the classroom as important as teaching reading (2010). Writing is now receiving new emphasis in high-stakes testing. Every teacher is expected to be a teacher of writing. Students are expected to write in school every day. The former trend of having students do mostly narrative writing in elementary school has given way to equal emphasis on informational and argumentative/opinion genres. There is newfound emphasis in Writing Across the Curriculum, which includes learning to write in the disciplines as well as Writing to Learn. We have delved deeply into each of these new directions in writing instruction in *Fostering Writing in Today's Classroom*, but other trends in writing are gaining national momentum.

One unexpected new trend is an early emphasis on teaching manuscript writing and the possible resurgence of teaching cursive handwriting, which was thought to be disappearing from schools. "Cursive Handwriting Disappearing from Public Schools," an article by T. Rees Shapiro and Sarah Voisin, shows the intensity of the debate on this important issue of writing instruction (2013). The curlicue letters of cursive handwriting, once considered a mainstay of American elementary education, have been slowly disappearing from classrooms for years. Media attention such as this has intensified the debate. But are manuscript and cursive handwriting really disappearing? The experts disagree.

Some experts argue that cursive handwriting is a dying craft. They say typing and word processing are replacing handwriting, which is often characterized as "an art" or merely a nice social and cultural tradition but is not very practical in today's digital world (Shapiro and Voisin 2013). There is no doubt that teaching writing in cursive is on the downswing over the last two decades. The main reason educators give for its decline is the time needed for instruction. While the delivery of content in schools that adopt Common Core State Standards and the like are often left to teachers or made on the local, state, and district levels, time for handwriting instruction in many locales has been replaced with time for teaching students how to use technology and time for state test preparation. Teachers are often left to pick and choose what to teach and feel buried with competing demands for instructional time.

At the opposite end of the spectrum, some experts see handwriting as making a comeback. Research on both manuscript and cursive writing, along with legislative action in a number of states, have recently come out in favor of handwriting instruction. Countries like Great Britain are bringing back handwriting even in the face of new technology for writing. In 2013, psychologist Angela Webb, Chairperson of the UK's National Handwriting Association, gave the following report, "In primary and most secondary schools (in the UK), keyboarding has hardly replaced handwriting at all for class assignments or exams.... Currently, 50–60 percent of the primary school day is spent on pen and paper activities, and all public exams are required to be handwritten at secondary and tertiary level, which is also true of most professional exams, such as accountancy, law and medicine" (Sawers 2013).

Perhaps one of the most important justifications for handwriting instruction comes from neuroscience and newfound brain scan connections between learning to write and learning to read. Dr. Karin Harman James, researcher at Indiana University, Department of Psychology and Brain Sciences, reported that "through a series of studies using functional Magnetic Resonance Imaging (fMRI) to probe how the brain processes stimuli in real time, we have demonstrated that, a) there is a distinct system in the human brain that is recruited during reading that is also recruited during writing, b) that the reading network develops as a function of handwriting experience, and c) that handwriting, and not keyboarding, leads to adult-like neural processing in the visual system of the preschool child. These findings suggest that self-generated action, in the form of handwriting, is a crucial component in setting up brain systems for reading acquisition. There is support for the notion that handwriting instruction is positively connected to learning to read" (2012, 1).

This study and others support a growing trend recognizing that teaching writing helps beginners learn to read with practical applications (Gentry and Peha 2013). Gentry and Peha recall the powerful precedent of Maria Montessori (1870–1952) who observed that children as young as two years of age were interested in tracing sandpaper letters and that many learned to write before reading. Even though learning to read English with its complex and "opaque" spelling system is harder than learning to read Montessori's native Italian, both research and practice reveal that many English speaking three- to six- year-olds write first and read later (Chomsky 1971; Gentry 2010).

Gentry and Peha (2013) provide the following five reasons why writing helps early reading:

1. **Early writing helps students crack the reading code.** Because our language is a sound-symbol system, early writers are practicing phonics when they attempt to write the sounds they hear. This practice combines segmenting and blending, the two fundamental early reading skills, into one purposeful activity.

2. **The first words students read are often the first ones they write**. Early writing builds reading confidence. Writing first helps students get the meaning connection because they are conveying their own thoughts in print with symbols for sounds.

3. **Writing gives students a head start on handwriting, spelling, punctuation, and other concepts of print.** Learning to write early on means students get more chances to practice handwriting, to learn to spell, to learn to punctuate, and to think about many of the conventions of printed text that are required to become successful readers. These include writing words left to right and lines top to bottom, putting spaces between words, and understanding the relationship between words and pictures. Early writing then becomes a form of self-testing, distributed practice, and interleaved practice of concepts of print and conventions— learning techniques that psychologists have found to be effective.

4. **Writing is a brainpower workout.** At a time when students' brainpower is growing extremely rapidly, writing may be the single best brain workout they can get for literacy. It requires all the skills of reading, some of the logical skills of mathematics and science, small-motor coordination, and even some emotional intelligence when young writers begin to consider writing for an audience.

5. **Writing is a useful assessment of reading ability.** Research shows that beginning reading and writing "are one and the same, almost" (Ehri 1997, 237). Teachers and parents can assess a student's early reading development and monitor progress by looking at their writing (Gentry 2010).

Gentry and Peha (2013a) follow through with the following five new trends for parents and preschool and kindergarten teachers to promote early writing (and reading) instruction:

- Give young students writing tools and encourage them to use them.

- Have beginners watch when you write, especially when you write simple things such as lists, and show them how to sound out words as you write.

- Have beginners practice writing the alphabet letters for fluency. Even if they can only form a few of the letters, have them practice writing them. Start with the lowercase letters because over 95 percent of the letters encountered in print are lowercase. Lowercase letters also take longer to learn, so students need more time to learn them.

- Have children write thank-you notes when they receive gifts. It's a wonderful habit for students to develop, and it gives them a real reason to write to a real person. Engage beginners in other real-life writing activities.

- Consider inviting beginners to copy their favorite stories or sections of stories from favorite books. Young writers build stamina for writing when they choose to do this activity and are able to read back their own writing. This gives them a sense of confidence and accomplishment.

Trend for Low-Stakes or No-Stakes Testing

Scores of research studies support the notion that testing improves learning, but testing may currently be getting a bad rap. Instead of focusing obsessively on high-stakes testing, which is expensive, time consuming, and often viewed as being of limited value for improving learning, there is a need to focus more on a kinder and gentler testing trend—no-stakes or low-stakes testing for learning. Testing that is completed as low-stakes or no-stakes is simply practice testing that is not graded. It includes short quizzes and daily assessment checks and writing for learning.

A recent influential study completed a comprehensive review of research on ten basic learning techniques. Self-testing and taking practice tests was one of the most highly-effective procedures for improved learning. The study pointed out that testing for learning need not be high-stakes testing; it can be taking a self-test or practice test or even writing down one's own thinking about how one solved a problem. In the study, other highly effective learning techniques that students could engage in by writing included *self-explanation* which involves recording the steps taken in solving a problem, or it could be writing to show how new information relates to one's prior knowledge (Dunlosky et al. 2013).

The study also found interleaved practice to be effective. Interleaved practice is a learning technique that involves varied, variable, or mixed practice, which is just the opposite of the often used *blocked practice* technique, which focuses on learning one skill at a time. Writing is a form of interleaved practice because it affords the student the opportunity to practice many skills in one purposeful activity. Kindergarten writers, for example, engage in interleaved practice when they write by practicing and alternating a variety of skills: sounding out words, making letters, making letter-sound correspondences, spelling, making the voice-to-print match, orienting print on the page, exploring the concept of what a word is, and the like.

Trend for Brain-Based and Science-Based Learning

New directions in writing instruction include a trend for evidence-based learning. We continue to find a growing research based for the practices and techniques that we espouse in *Fostering Writing in Today's Classroom*. One interesting example in which new science is supporting what we consider to be best practice is in process writing.

In Chapter 3, we explained how the late Donald Graves founded the Process Writing Laboratory at the University of New Hampshire in 1976 and conducted research in the classroom that led to a worldwide revolution in writing instruction. In doing so, he discovered three keys to motivate writers: choice of topic, giving the child ownership, and writing for a real audience. There is a growing evidence base for Graves's (1984) thoughts about motivation, and his thoughts are as fresh and inspirational today as they were when he began his research project.

Best-selling author Daniel Pink makes a strong science-based case for essentially the same three motivational factors that Graves (1984) listed: choice of topic, ownership, and a real audience (2010). Pink calls them (1) autonomy, (2) mastery, and (3) purpose, and he says they lead to "better performance and personal satisfaction." Autonomy, mastery, and purpose are qualities we should take seriously with all students as writers. Take a moment to think about each of these motivators for writers in the Graves context:

Choice of Topic (Autonomy): Pink (2010) says autonomy is our desire to be self-directed, which leads to engagement. Giving students a choice in writing fits the need to be self-directed.

Ownership (Mastery): Ownership and mastery are two peas in the same pod. Graves famously pointed out that "kids want to write!" They want to own the ability to write and the ability to read back what they have written. As you engage your students as writers, giving them ownership leads to mastery. They begin to master the fundamentals and feel successful. According to Pink (2010) this mastery creates the urge to get better.

Real Audience (Purpose): Students engage in the purpose motive when they write for a real purpose and a real audience. It may start in kindergarten as students make a grocery list or when they send a "thank you" note to a real person. The purpose motive follows the writer throughout school and into adulthood.

Make it your goal to bestow autonomy, mastery, and purpose in your student writers, and watch their motivation to write grow. Don't ask, "How do I motivate my students to write?" Both Donald Graves and Daniel Pink (2010) have given us the answer. Ask, "How do I increase each student's sense of autonomy, mastery, and purpose as a writer?"

Switching Gears: From Marking Errors to Praise, Encouragement, and Support

It's often the struggling writer that teachers find most difficult to motivate, and sometimes we need to switch gears. It's easy to look at a piece of student writing wracked with errors and think that the situation is hopeless. When you find yourself in this situation, turn the tables and look on the bright side. The following tips for motivating struggling writers demonstrate how little steps and positive thinking can turn things around.

Tips for Motivating Struggling Writers

> **Begin with a positive attitude.** Envision success in your struggling writers. Be hopeful and excited about the impact that your manner, words, and teaching can have on a student's writing growth.

> **Praise and encourage.** Often, struggling writers become easily frustrated as their peers' accomplishments are recognized and celebrated. Be especially attentive to even the slightest improvement made by struggling writers. Provide frequent praise by reminding students how proud they should be of their accomplishments (e.g., "You must be so proud of your effort and perseverance"). Giving encouragement in an environment where all writers are valued will motivate your struggling writers.

➤ **Be an active observer.** When you "teach from your feet, not from your seat," you become engaged in monitoring, encouraging, and supporting your students' efforts. As you move about the classroom, notice students who are struggling. Move in, compliment their efforts, and direct them step by step through any difficult writing task.

➤ **Provide choice and purpose.** When we offer all students choice in selecting their writing topics and creating authentic purposes for writing, we give ownership and value to the writing tasks. For struggling writers, generating topic ideas and determining the purpose of their writing can be overwhelming. Take time to confer individually or in a small group to ask open-ended questions to probe and elicit a list of possible writing topics that are personally interesting to that student. Discuss and chart the audience and purpose for the writing that is relative to the student's interest. Supporting struggling writers with topic choice and writing purpose lessens the anxiety and motivates them to begin their writing tasks.

➤ **Be their "guide on the side."** Anytime something new is attempted, it is comforting to know that someone who has accomplished the task can answer questions, guide you if you become confused, and provide additional resources to support your efforts. (Think about when you were the "new" teacher.) We are that person for our struggling writers. We guide them through achievable goals, supporting them with small steps, such as breaking a writing task into smaller parts that are more easily accomplished. Small steps might be guiding a writer by placing his or her hand on yours to help them get started after you say, "Tell me what you want to say!" First you start writing what they want to say, then remove your hand, give them the pen, and say, "There you go. Keep writing!" Provide additional resources to meet their needs such as personal word banks, simplified anchor charts, graphic organizers, and mentor texts so that they are better equipped to accomplish their writing. Struggling writers soon recognize your genuine interest in their success.

➤ **Create opportunities for collaboration.** Providing collaborative opportunities for small, heterogeneous groups reminds students that when we help each other, we help ourselves. These small groups are often helpful and supportive to struggling writers as peer mentors provide different aptitudes, talents, and attitudes. Collaboration time to reflect on accomplishments can increase the confidence of struggling writers and motivate them to set new goals for writing success. Planning collaborative time with colleagues gives you time to share instructional practices, discuss students' progress, and generate ideas to continually improve your writers' development and motivation. Set time aside to collaborate with parents as well. A quick phone call, a personal note, or a scheduled conference to share a struggling writer's accomplishments lets students know you not only value them as a writer but you also value them as your student. Just think how motivated we become when the people dearest to us recognize our successes!

Reflect and Review

1. Reflect on your craft. Based on this chapter, what new directions will you take for writing instruction in your classroom? List your goals for this year. Consider technology, handwriting, low-stakes testing, high-stakes testing, and motivation.

2. What other writing "new directions" are currently being discussed in the education realm? With your colleagues, discuss ways you can support each other in the writing classroom as you address these issues.

3. How are you following new trends or evidenced-based learning in your teaching practices?

4. How are you increasing each student's use of autonomy, mastery, and purpose as a writer?

5. In what ways can the use of technology not only support your writing instruction but also inspire and enhance student learning?

Afterword

Passion and Perseverance

Writing is a complex process, not just for the learner but also for the teacher. Our intent, as we brainstormed the content of this book was, and still is, to provide the essential tools to support, enhance, and foster writing in the classroom.

We have demonstrated how to create an environment that applauds and celebrates risks, where writers are encouraged, guided, and supported. We have shown you materials and management procedures to facilitate your teaching and student learning. We have shown you the connection between writer's workshop and the writing process and the essential role each plays in the teaching of writing. We have shown you the importance of teaching your students to value writing as a means to express, to learn, to question, to explore, to entertain, and to create not only across the curriculum but also in life, for real-world purposes and audiences. We have shown you how the language of the traits of quality writing can inspire your students to think, read, and talk like a writer.

Each of the above represents best practices in the teaching of writing, but best practices alone may not be enough. We believe that you, the teacher, holds the key to your students' success in writing. It is your knowledge about them as writers, belief and respect for them as writers, and encouragement that motivates your students as writers. Turn that key, not only with best practices but also with passion and perseverance.

Your passion motivates you to commit the time, energy, and teaching necessary to develop an effective writer's workshop where students are excited and enthusiastic about writing. Your passion guides your commitment to teaching, guiding, monitoring, and conferencing with your student writers. Sometimes writing instruction will be a challenge. It requires perseverance to pursue and accomplish goals. Know that your perseverance and commitment will not be in vain.

Foster writing in your classroom with best practices. Let your passion and perseverance inspire and help your students become the best writers they can be. Remember these inspirational words of our mentor, Donald Graves: "Think of how many teachers you had who actually helped you with your writing. Most people can name one or two. I say to teachers, 'Be that one teacher for a child!'"

References Cited

Allal, Linda. 1997. "Learning to Spell in the Classroom." In *Learning to Spell: Research, Theory, and Practice Across Languages*, edited by Charles A. Perfetti, Laurence Rieben, and Michel Fayol, 131–137. Hillsdale, NJ: Lawrence Erlbaum Associates.

Anderson, Carl. 2001. *How's It Going? A Practical Guide to Conferring with Student Writers*. Portsmouth, NH: Heinemann.

Anderson, Rebecca, Michael M. Grant, and Bruce W. Speck. 2008. *Technology to Teach Literacy: A Resource for K–8 Teachers*. Upper Saddle River, NJ: Pearson Education, Inc.

Angelillo, Janet. 2005. *Writing to the Prompt: When Students Don't Have a Choice*. Portsmouth, NH: Heinemann.

Arnosky, Jim. 2002. *All About Rattlesnakes*. New York, NY: Scholastic.

Atwell, Nancie. 1990. *Coming to Know: Writing to Learn in the Intermediate Grades*. Portsmouth, NH: Heinemann.

———. 1998. *In the Middle: New Understandings About Writing, Reading, and Learning*. Portsmouth, NH: Heinemann.

———. 2008. Foreword. In *Day-to-Day Assessment in the Reading Workshop: Making Informed Instructional Decisions in Grades 3–6*. New York, NY: Scholastic.

Baylor, Byrd. 1985. *Everybody Needs a Rock*. Chicago, IL: Aladdin Publishing.

———. 1998. *The Table Where Rich People Sit*. Chicago, IL: Aladdin Publishing.

Bear, Donald R., Marcia A. Invernizzi, Shane Templeton, and Francine Johnston. 2012. *Words Their Way (5th Edition)*. New York, NY: Pearson.

Beers, Kylene, and Robert E. Probst. 2013. *Notice & Note: Strategies for Close Reading*. Portsmouth, NH: Heinemann.

Bellamy, Peter. 2005. *Seeing with New Eyes: Using the 6+1 Trait® Writing Model*. Portland, OR: NW Regional Educational Laboratory.

Berninger, Virginia W. 2012. "Evidence-Based, Developmentally Appropriate Writing Skills K–5: Teaching the Orthographic Loop of Working Memory to Write Letters So Developing Writers Can Spell Words and Express Ideas." Accessed February 25. https://www.hw21summit.com/media/zb/hw21/H2937N_Berninger_presentation.pdf.

Blair, Nancye. 2012. "Technology Integration for the New 21st Century Learner." Accessed February 25. http://www.naesp.org/principal-januaryfebruary-2012-technology/technology-integration-new-21st-century-learner.

Calkins, Lucy. 1982. "Writing Taps a New Energy Source: The Child." In *Donald Graves in Australia*, edited by Walshe, R.D., XX. Rozelle, NSW, Australia: Primary English Teaching Association.

———. 1994. *The Art of Teaching Writing*. Portsmouth, NH: Heinemann.

———. 2003. *The Conferring Handbook*. Portsmouth, NH: Heinemann.

Calkins, Lucy, and Marjorie Martinelli. 2006. *Launching the Writing Workshop*. Portsmouth, NH: Heinemann.

Cannon, Janell. 1993. *Stellaluna*. New York, NY: Harcourt Brace & Company.

Carnesi, Sabrina, and Karen DiGiorgio. 2009. "Teaching the Inquiry Process to 21st Century Learners." Accessed February 25. http://www.librarymediaconnection.com/pdf/lmc/reviews_and_articles/featured_articles/Carnesi_March_April2009.pdf.

Chomsky, Carol. 1971. "Write First, Read Later." *Childhood Education* 47: 296–300.

Christy, Janice. 2005. "High Stakes Testing in the Classroom." Accessed February 27. http://www.glencoe.com/sec/teachingtoday/subject/writing_portfolios.phtml.

———. 2013. "Writing Portfolios for a High Stakes Testing World." Accessed February 27. http://www.glencoe.com/sec/teachingtoday/subject/writing_portfolios.phtml.

Culham, Ruth. 2003. *6 + 1 Traits of Writing: The Complete Guide: Grades 3 and Up*. New York, NY: Scholastic.

Cunningham, Patricia M., and James W. Cunningham. 2010. *What Really Matters in Writing: Research-Based Practices across the Elementary Curriculum.* Boston, MA: Pearson Education, Inc.

Dahl, Roald, and Quentin Blake. 1998. *The Twits.* New York, NY: Puffin Books.

Daniels, Harvey, and Marilyn Bizar. 2004. *Teaching the Best Practice Way.* Portland, ME: Stenhouse Publishers.

Davies, Nicola, and Jane Chapman. 2001. *One Tiny Turtle.* Cambridge, MA: Candlewick Press.

Davis, Judy, and Sharon Hill. 2003. *The No-Nonsense Guide to Teaching Writing.* Portsmouth, NH: Heinemann.

Dierking, Connie Campbell, and Sherra Jones. 2003. *Growing Up Writing: Mini-Lessons for Emergent and Beginning Writers.* Gainesville, FL: Maupin House.

Dorn, Linda J., and Carla Soffos. 2001. *Scaffolding Young Writers: A Writers' Workshop Approach.* Portland, ME: Stenhouse Publishers.

Duffy, Mary L., Joanna Jones, and Susan W. Thomas. 1999. "Using Portfolios to Foster Independent Thinking." *Intervention in School and Clinic* 35 (1): 34–37.

Dunlosky, John, Katherine A. Rawson, Elizabeth J. Marsh, Mitchell J. Nathan, and Daniel T. Willingham. 2013. "Improving Students' Learning with Effective Learning Techniques: Promising Directions from Cognitive and Educational Psychology." *Psychological Science in the Public Interest* 14 (1): 4–58.

Dyson, Anne Haas, and Sarah Warshauer Freedman. 1990. "On Teaching Writing: A Review of the Literature." National Center for the Study of Writing. Accessed on February 28, 2014. http://www.nwp.org/cs/public/download/nwp_file/111/OP20.pdf?x-r=pcfile_d.

Egawa, Kathy. n.d. "Writing in the Early Grades, K–2." National Council of Teachers of English. Accessed February 28, 2014. http://www.ncte.org/writing/aboutearlygrades.

———. 1998. "Writing in the Middle Grades, 6–8." National Council of Teachers of English. Accessed August 23, 2004. http:// www.ncte.org/prog/writing/research/113177.htm.

Ehri, Linnea. 1994. *Landmark Essays on Voice and Writing*. New York, NY: Routledge.

———. 1997. "Learning to Read and Learning to Spell Are One and the Same, Almost." In *Learning to Spell: Research, Theory and Practice Across Languages*, edited by Charles A. Perfetti, Laurence Rieben, and Michel Fayol, 237–269. New York, NY: Routledge.

———. 2000. "Learning to Read and Learning to Spell: Two Sides of the Same Coin." *Topics in Learning Disorders* 20: 19–49.

Elbow, Peter. 1998. *Writing Without Teachers (2nd Edition)*. New York, NY: Oxford University Press.

Fleming, Nora. 2012. "Latest NAEP Test Assesses Computer-Based Writing." *Education Week*. Accessed October 4, 2013. http://www.edweek.org/dd/articles/2012/10/17/01bits-naep.h06.html.

Fletcher, Ralph. 1996. *A Writer's Notebook: Unlocking the Writer Within You*. New York, NY: HarperCollins.

———. 1997. *Twilight Comes Twice*. New York, NY: Clarion Books.

———. 2000. *How Writers Work: Finding a Process that Works for You*. New York, NY: HarperCollins Publishers.

———. 2010. *Pyrotechnics on the Page: Playful Craft that Sparks Writing*. Portland, ME: Stenhouse Publishers.

Fountas, Irene C., and Gay Su Pinnell. 2001. *Guiding Readers and Writers Grades 3–6*. Portsmouth, NH: Heinemann.

Fox, Mem. 1993. *Radical Reflections: Passionate Opinions on Teaching, Learning, and Living*. New York, NY: Harcourt Brace and Company.

Gentry, Richard J. 2004. *The Science of Spelling*. Portsmouth, NH: Heinemann.

———. 2006. *Breaking the Code: The New Science of Beginning Reading and Writing*. Portsmouth, NH: Heinemann.

———. 2010. *Raising Confident Readers: How to Teach Your Child to Read and Write—from Baby to Age 7*. Boston, MA: Da Capo/Lifelong Press.

————. 2013a. "5 Reasons Why Writing Helps Early Reading" *Psychology Today* (blog), September 15. Accessed February 28, 2014. http://www.psychologytoday.com/blog/raising-readers-writers-and-spellers/201309/5-reasons-why-writing-helps-early-reading.

————. 2013b. "5 Learning Techniques Psychologists Say Kids Aren't Getting in School." *Psychology Today* (blog), July 9. Accessed February 28, 2014. http://www.psychologytoday.com/blog/raising-readers-writers-and-spellers/201307/5-learning-techniques-psychologists-say-kids-aren-t.

Gentry, Richard, Jan McNeel, and Vickie Wallace-Nesler. 2012a. *Getting to the Core of Writing Level K*. Huntington Beach, CA: Shell Education.

————. 2012b. *Getting to the Core of Writing Level 1*. Huntington Beach, CA: Shell Education.

————. 2012c. *Getting to the Core of Writing Level 2*. Huntington Beach, CA: Shell Education.

————. 2012d. *Getting to the Core of Writing Level 3*. Huntington Beach, CA: Shell Education.

————. 2012e. *Getting to the Core of Writing Level 4*. Huntington Beach, CA: Shell Education.

————. 2012f. *Getting to the Core of Writing Level 5*. Huntington Beach, CA: Shell Education.

————. 2013g. *Getting to the Core of Writing Level 6*. Huntington Beach, CA: Shell Education.

Graham, Steve, and Michael Hebert. 2012. "Writing to Read: Evidence for How Writing Can Improve Reading." Carnegie Corporation of New York. Accessed on February 28, 2014. http://carnegie.org/fileadmin/Media/Publications/WritingToRead_01.pdf.

Graves, Donald. 1983. *Writing: Teachers and Children at Work*. Portsmouth, NH: Heinemann.

————. 1985. "All Children Can Write." LD Online. Accessed September 22, 2013. http://www.ldonline.org/article/6204/.

————. 1994. *A Fresh Look at Writing*. Portsmouth, NH: Heinemann.

Hamilton, Boni. 2007. *It's Elementary! Integrating Technology in the Primary Grades.* Washington, DC: ISTE Publications.

Hart Research Associates. 2010. "Raising the Bar: Employers' Views on College Learning in the Wake of the Economic Downturn." Association of American Colleges and Universities by Hart Research Associates. Accessed February 28, 2014. https://www.aacu.org/leap/documents/2009_EmployerSurvey.pdf.

Heard, Georgia. 1995. *Writing Toward Home: Tales and Lessons to Find Your Way.* Portsmuth, NH: Heinemann Publishing.

Hicks, Troy. "Digital Writing with Troy Hicks." *Choice Literacy* video. June 2011. http://www.choiceliteracy.com/articles-detail-view.php?id=1021.

Higgins, Betty, Melinda Miller, and Susan Wegmann. 2006. "Teaching to the Test . . . Not! Balancing Best Practice and Testing Requirements in Writing." *The Reading Teacher* 60 (4): 310–319.

Howard, Rachel. "Gesture Writing." *The New York Times*, May 26, 2013.

Invernizzi, Marcia, Mary Abouzeid, and J. Thomas Gill. 1994. "Using Students' Invented Spellings as a Guide for Spelling Instruction that Emphasizes Word Study." *Elementary School Journal* 95 (2):155–167.

James, Karin Harman. 2012. "The Neural Correlates of Handwriting and Its Affect on Reading Acquisition." Paper presented at Handwriting in the 21st century? *An Educational Summit*, Washington, D.C., January 23, 2012.

James, Karin Harman, and Laura Engelhardt. 2013. "The Effects of Handwriting Experience on Functional Brain Development in Pre-literate Children." *Trends in Neuroscience and Education* 1 (1): 32–42.

Kennedy, X.J. 2013. *An Introduction to Poetry.* London, England: Longman Publishing.

Kennedy, X.J., and Dorothy. 1999. *Knock A Star. A Child's Introduction to Poetry.* New York, NY: Little, Brown Books for Young Readers.

Kuklthau, Carol C., Leslie K. Maniotes, and Ann K. Caspari. 2007. *Guided Inquiry: Learning in the 21st Century.* Westport, CT & London: Libraries Unlimited.

Langer, Judith A., and Arthur N. Applebee. 1987. *How Writing Shapes Thinking: A Study of Teaching and Learning.* Urbana, IL: National Council of Teachers of English.

Lehman, Christopher, and Kate Roberts. 2013. *Falling in Love with Close Reading: Lessons for Analyzing Texts and Life.* Portsmouth, NH: Heinemann.

Lensmire, Timothy J. 1998. "Rewriting Student Voice." *Journal of Curriculum Studies* 30 (3): 261–291.

Lester, Julius. 1994. *John Henry.* New York, NY: Dial Books.

Mermelstein, Leah. 2007. *Don't Forget to Share: The Crucial Last Step in the Writing Workshop.* Portsmouth, NH: Heinemann.

Minkel, Justin. 2013. "Lions, Tigers, and Mating Polar Bears, Oh My! 2nd Grade Researchers Writing to Read." *Education Week Teacher* (blog), December 8. Accessed on February 28, 2014. http://blogs.edweek.org /teachers/teaching_for_triumph/2013/12/lions_tigers_and_mating _polar_.html.

Murray, Donald. 2004. *Write to Learn.* Stamford, CT: Cengage Learning.

Myers, Walter Dean. 1996. *Slam!* New York, NY: Scholastic.

National Commission on Writing. 2003. "The Neglected 'R': The Need for a Writing Revolution." National Writing Project. Accessed September 18, 2013. http://www.nwp.org/cs/public/print/ resource/2523.

National Council of Teachers of English Task Force on Writing Assessment. 2013. "NCTE Position Statement on Machine Scoring." NCTE. Accessed October 1, 2013. http://www.ncte.org/positions/statements /machine_scoring.

National Governors Association Center for Best Practices, Council of Chief State School Officers. 2010. "Common Core State Standards." National Governors Association Center for Best Practices. Accessed on February 28, 2014. http://www.corestandards.org/the-standards.

National Writing Project with DeVoss, Danielle Nicole, Elyse Eidman-Aadahl, and Troy Hicks. 2010. *Because Digital Writing Matters: Improving Student Writing in Online and Multimedia Environments.* San Francisco, CA: Jossey-Bass, A Wiley Imprint.

Northwest Regional Educational Laboratory. 2005. *Seeing with New Eyes: A Guidebook on Teaching and Assessing Beginning Writers Using the Six-Trait Writing Model*, 6th ed. Portland, OR: Northwest Regional Educational Laboratory.

Norton, Elizabeth S., Ioulia Kovelman, and Laura-Ann Petitto. 2007. "Are There Separate Neural Systems for Spelling? New Insights into the Role of Rules and Memory in Spelling from Functional Magnetic Resonance Imaging." *Mind Brain and Education* 1 (1): 48–59.

Oates, Joyce Carol. Accessed on July 19, 2013. http://www.goodreads.com/quotes/851275-getting-the-first-draft-finished-is-like-pushing-a-very.

Peha, Steve. 2013a. "5 Learning Techniques Psychologists Say Kids Aren't Getting in School." *Psychology Today* (blog), July 9. Accessed February 28, 2014.

———. 2013b. "Welcome to Writer's Workshop. "Accessed October 4, 2013. http://www.ttms.org/PDFs/05%20writers%20workshop%20vool%20(Full)pdf.

———. 2013c. "Writing Across the Curriculum." Teaching that Makes Sense. Accessed February 28, 2014. http://www.ttms.org/PDFs/06%20Writing%20Across%20the%20Curriculum%20v001%20(Full).pdf.

Pink, Daniel H. 2010. *Drive: The Surprising Truth About What Motivates Us.* New York, NY: Riverhead Books.

Portalupi, JoAnn, and Ralph Fletcher. 1998. *Craft Lessons: Teaching Writing K–8.* Portland, ME: Stenhouse Publishers.

Ray, Katie Wood. 2002. *What You Know by Heart: How to Develop Curriculum for Your Writing Workshop.* Portsmouth, NH: Heinemann.

Ray, Katie Wood, and Lester L. Laminack. 2001. *The Writing Workshop.* Urbana, Illinois: National Council of Teachers of English.

Routman, Regie. 2005. *Writing Essentials: Raising Expectations and Results While Simplifying Teaching.* Portsmouth, NH: Heinemann.

Ryan, Pam Munoz. 2003. *Hello Ocean.* Watertown, MA: Charlesbridge Publishing.

Santangelo, T., and S. Graham. 2011. "Does Explicit Spelling Instruction Make Students Better Spellers, Readers, and Writers?" Poster presented at the Pacific Coast Research Conference, Coronado, CA, 2011.

Sawers, Paul. 2013. "The Future of Handwriting." *The Next Web* (blog), August 30. Accessed February 28, 2014. http://thenextweb.com/insider/2013/08/30/the-future-of-handwriting/.

Schenone, Ron. 2012. "Robo-Graders: How Accurate Are They?" *LockerGnome* (blog), October 4. Accessed February 28, 2014. http://www.lockergnome.com/blade/2012/04/30/robo-graders-how-accurate-are-they/.

Schlagal, Bob. 2002. "Classroom Spelling Instruction: History, Research, and Practice." *Reading Research and Instruction* 42 (1): 44–50.

Schwartz, Susan. 1991. *Creating the Child-Centered Classroom*. Katonah, NY: Richard C. Owen Publishers, Inc.

Shanahan, Timothy. 2012. "What Is Close Reading?" Accessed February 28, 2014. http://www.shanahanonliteracy.com/2012/06/what-is-close-reading.html.

Shapiro, T. Rees, and Sarah L. Voisin. 2013. "Cursive Handwriting Disappearing from Public Schools." Accessed February 28, 2014. http://articles.washingtonpost.com/2013-04-04/local/38274984_1_cursive-students-districts.

Sharp, Ann C., Gale M. Sinatra, and Ralph E. Reynolds. 2008. "The Development of Children's Orthographic Knowledge: A Microgenetic Perspective." *Reading Research Quarterly* 43 (3): 206–226.

Spandel, Vicki. 2008. *Creating Young Writers: Using the Six Traits to Enrich Writing Process in Primary Classrooms (2nd Edition)*. New York, NY: Allyn and Bacon.

Sperling, Melanie, and Deborah Appleman. 2011. "Voice in the Context of Literacy Studies." *Reading Research Quarterly* 46 (1): 70–84.

Vygotsky, Lev S. 1978. *In Mind in Society: The Development of Higher Psychological Processes*, edited by Michael Cole, Vera John-Steiner, Sylvia Scribner, and Ellen Souberman. Cambridge, MA: Harvard Universtiy Press.

Wallace, Robert. 2011. *Writing Poems*. London, England: Longman Publishing.

Walshe, Robert Daniel. 1981. "Children Want to Write." In *Donald Graves in Australia*: Rozelle, NSW, Australia: Primary English Teaching Association.

———. 1982. *Donald Graves in Australia*. Rozelle, NSW, Australia: Primary English Teaching Association.

Weaver, Constance. 2008. *Grammar to Enrich and Enhance Writing*. Portsmouth, NH: Heinemann.

Welty, Eudora. 1994. *A Writer's Eye*. Jackson, MS: University Press of Mississippi.

Wilde, Sandra. 1999. "How Children Learn to Spell." In *Voices on Word Matters*, edited by Irene Fountas and Gay Su Pinnell, 173–178. Portsmouth, NH: Heinemann.

Wolf, Shelby Ann, and Kenneth Paul Wolf. 2002. "Teaching True and To the Test in Writing." California State University, Northridge. Accessed September 24, 2013. http://www.csun.edu/~krowlands/Content /Academic_Resources/Composition/writing_on_demand/Wolf-%20 teaching%20true%20to%20the%20test.pdf.

Recommended Reading

Chapter 1

Armstrong, Jennifer. 2006. *The American Story: 100 True Tales from American History*. New York, NY: Random House Children's Books.

Buckner, Aimee. 2005. *Notebook Know How: Strategies for the Writer's Notebook*. Portland, ME: Stenhouse Publishers.

Denenburg, Denise. 2005. *50 American Heroes Every Kid Should Meet*. Minneapolis, MN: Millbrook Press.

Fletcher, Ralph. 1996. *A Writer's Notebook: Unlocking the Writer Within You*. New York, NY: HarperCollins Publishers.

Fountas, Irene C., and Gay Su Pinnell. 2001. *Guiding Readers and Writers Grades 3–6*. Portsmouth, NH: Heinemann.

Lionni, Leo. 1973. *Swimmy*. New York, NY: Random House.

Ray, Katie Wood, and Lester L. Laminack. 2001. *The Writing Workshop*. Urbana, IL: National Council of Teachers of English.

Seymour, Simon. 2009. Smithsonian Collins Series. New York, NY: HarperCollins Publishers

Slaughter, Holly. 2009. *Small-Group Writing Conferences: How to Use Your Instructional Time More Efficiently*. Portsmouth, NH: Heinemann.

Chapter 2

Anderson, Carl. 2000. *How's It Going? A Practical Guide to Conferring with Student Writers*. Portsmouth, NH: Heinemann.

Calkins, Lucy, Amanda Hartman, and Zoe Ryder White. 2005. *One to One: The Art of Conferring with Young Writers*. Portsmouth, NH: Heinemann.

Fletcher, Ralph, and JoAnn Portalupi. 2001. *Writing Workshop: The Essential Guide*. Portsmouth, NH: Heinemann.

Ray, Katie Wood, and Lester L. Laminack. 2001. *The Writing Workshop*. Urbana, IL: National Council of Teachers of English.

Chapter 3

Graves, Donald. 1983. *Writing: Teachers and Children at Work*. Portsmouth NH: Heinemann.

Walshe, Robert Daniel. 1982. *Donald Graves in Australia*. Rozelle, NSW, Australia: Primary English Teaching Association.

Chapter 4

Gentry, Richard. 2006. *Breaking the Code: The New Science of Beginning Reading and Writing*. Portsmouth, NH: Heinemann.

———. 2010. *Raising Confident Readers: How to Teach Your Child to Read and Write—from Baby to Age 7*. Boston, MA: Da Capo/Lifelong Press.

Chapter 5

Atwell, Nancie. 1990. *Coming to Know: Writing to Learn in the Intermediate Grades*. Portsmouth, NH: Heinemann.

———. 1998. *In the Middle: New Understandings About Writing, Reading, and Learning*. Portsmouth, NH: Heinemann.

———. 1990. *Coming to Know: Writing to Learn in the Intermediate Grades*. Portsmouth, NH: Heinemann.

Beers, Kylene, and Robert E. Probst. 2013. *Notice & Note: Strategies for Close Reading*. Portsmouth, NH: Heinemann.

Peha, Steve. 2013. "Writing Across the Curriculum." Teaching that Makes Sense. Accessed February 28, 2014. http://www.ttms.org/PDFs/06%20Writing%20Across%20the%20Curriculum%20v001%20(Full).pdf.

Chapter 6

Baylor, Byrd. 1985. *Everybody Needs a Rock*. New York, NY: Aladdin.

Baylor, Byrd. 1998. *The Table Where Rich People Sit*. New York, NY: Aladdin Picture Books.

Bellamy, Peter. 2005. *Seeing with New Eyes: Using the 6+1 Trait® Writing Model*. Portland, OR: Northwest Regional Educational Laboratory.

Brinckloe, Julie. 1986. *Fireflies*. New York, NY: Aladdin Books.

Bunting, Eve. 1993. *Fly Away Home*. Boston, MA: Houghton Mifflin Hartcourt.

Cannon, Janell. 1993. *Stellaluna*. Boston, MA: Houghton Mifflin Hartcourt.

Cannon. Janell. 2005. *Crickwing*. Boston, MA: Houghton Mifflin Hartcourt.

Fletcher, Ralph. 1996. *A Writer's Notebook: Unlocking the Writer Within You*. New York, NY: HarperCollins Publishers.

Gentry, Richard. 2004. *The Science of Spelling*. Portsmouth, NH: Heinemann.

Heard, Georgia. 1999 "Dragonfly." *Creatures of Earth, Sea, and Sky: Animal Poems*. Honesdale, PA: Boy Mills Press.

Henkes, Kevin. 2006. *Lily's Purple Plastic Purse*. New York, NY: Greenwillow Books.

Henkes, Kevin. 2008. *Chrysanthemum*. New York, NY: HarperCollins Publishers.

Hesse, Karen. 1998. *The Music of Dolphins*. New York, NY: Scholastic Paperbacks.

Mazer, Anne. 1994. *The Salamander Room*. New York, NY: Random House Children's Books.

Meyers, Walter Dean. 1998. *Slam!* New York, NY: Scholastic Paperbacks.

Munch, Robert. 2002. *Alligator Baby, 1st Edition*. New York, NY: Cartwheel.

Palatini, Margie. 2003. *Bedhead*. New York, NY: Simon and Schuster Books for Young Readers.

Paterson, Katherine. 2004. *Bridge to Terabethia*. New York, NY: HarperTeen.

Pretlutsky, Jack. "I Wish I Had a Dragon." *Dragons are Singing Tonight*. New York, NY: HarperCollins Publishers.

Pretlutsky, Jack. 1990. "My Neighbors Dog is Purple." *Something Big Has Been Here*. New York, NY: HarperCollins Publishers.

Rylant, Cynthia. 1985. *The Relatives Came*. New York, NY: Atheneum.

Silverstein, Shel. 1974. "One Sister for Sale." *Where the Sidewalk Ends*. New York, NY: HarperCollins Publishers.

Sperling, Melanie, and Deborah Appleman. 2011. "Voice in the Context of Literacy Studies." *Reading Research Quarterly* 46 (1): 70–84.

Spandel, Vicki. 2008. *Creating Young Writers: Using the Six Traits to Enrich Writing Process in Primary Classrooms (2nd Edition)*. New York, NY: Allyn & Bacon.

Steig, William. 2011. *Brave Irene*. New York, NY: Square Fish.

Steig, William. 2012. *Sylvester and the Magic Pebble*. New York, NY: Little Simon.

Van Allsburg, Chris. 1986. *The Stranger*. Boston, MA: Houghton Mifflin Hartcourt.

Winter, Jeanette. 1992. *Follow the Drinking Gourd*. New York, NY: Dragonfly Books.

Wood, Douglas. 2005. *A Quiet Place*. New York, NY: Simon and Schuster Books for Young Readers.

Yolen, Jane. 1987. *Owl Moon*. New York, NY: Philomel.

Yolen, Jane. 1991. *Greyling*. New York, NY: Philomel.

Chapter 7

Anderson, Rebecca, Michael M. Grant, and Bruce W. Speck. 2008. *Technology to Teach Literacy: A Resource for K–8 Teachers*. Upper Saddle River, NJ: Pearson Education, Inc.

Gentry, Richard. 2013a. "5 Learning Techniques Psychologists Say Kids Aren't Getting in School." *Psychology Today* (blog), July 9. Accessed February 28, 2014. http://www.psychologytoday.com/blog/raising-readers-writers-and-spellers/201307/5-learning-techniques-psychologists-say-kids-aren-t.

———. 2013b. "5 Reasons Why Writing Helps Early Reading" *Psychology Today* (blog), September 15. Accessed February 28, 2014. http://www.psychologytoday.com/blog/raising-readers-writers-and-spellers/201309/5-reasons-why-writing-helps-early-reading.

National Writing Project with DeVoss, Danielle Nicole, Elyse Eidman-Aadahl, and Troy Hicks. 2010. *Because Digital Writing Matters: Improving Student Writing in Online and Multimedia Environments*. San Francisco, CA: Jossey-Bass, A Wiley Imprint.

Peha, Steve. 2013. "5 Learning Techniques Psychologists Say Kids Aren't Getting in School." *Psychology Today* (blog), July 9. Accessed February 28, 2014.

Pink, Daniel H. 2010. *Drive: The Surprising Truth About What Motivates Us*. New York, NY: Riverhead Books.

Sawers, Paul. 2013. "The Future of Handwriting" *The Next Web* (blog), August 30. Accessed February 28, 2014. http://thenextweb.com/insider/2013/08/30/the-future-of-handwriting/.

Phase 0	(Preschool or sooner)
Spelling/Sound Awareness Looks Like:	No spelling May clap syllables May shout out rhyming words
Word Reading Looks Like:	Reads memorized sight words or phrases May pretend to read
Guided Reading Looks Like:	Responds to read-alouds with repeated readings and dialogue reading Memory reading of words and phrases and favorite books
Writing Looks Like:	Characterized by marking, drawing, and scribbling, leading to letter-like forms
Writing Sample:	

Phase 1	(First half of kindergarten or sooner)
Spelling/Sound Awareness Looks Like:	Writes letters but no attention to sounds Claps syllables Shouts out rhyming words No phonemic awareness in evidence
Word Reading Looks Like:	Reads envrionmental print Has little capacity to "sound out" Relies on pictures, logographic memory, or guessing Ehri's Pre-alphabetic Phase: Child sees *Crest®* and says *toothpaste*; sees the *golden arches* and says *McDonald's®*
Guided Reading Looks Like:	Memory reading of Level A easy books
Writing Looks Like:	Attempts to write messages and stories using letters
Writing Sample:	 **A flock of butterflies**

Phase 2	(End of kindergarten or sooner)
Spelling/Sound Awareness Looks Like:	Writes using beginning and ending letter-sound correspondences
Word Reading Looks Like:	Reads memorized sight words
	Cues words using beginning, ending, or prominent letters
	Ehri's Partial-alphabetic Phase: sees *ink* and says *ice*; sees *klug* and says *king*
Guided Reading Looks Like:	Memory reading of Level A-C easy books
Writing Looks Like:	Labels drawings or writes message with a few letter-sound matches
Writing Sample:	

Humpty Dumpty

Phase 3	(First half of first grade or sooner)
Spelling/Sound Awareness Looks Like:	Spells with a letter for each sound
	Has full phonemic awareness; e.g., *night* spelled NIT for /n/+/ī/+/t/; *came* spelled CAM for /k/+/ā/+/m/
Word Reading Looks Like:	Reads many more known sight words
	Ehri's Full-alphabetic Phase: Distinguishes similarly spelled words such as *king* and *kick*; uses knowledge of *pink* to figure out *ink*
Guided Reading Looks Like:	Memory reading of Level C-G easy books
Writing Looks Like:	Writes by attending to one letter for each sound
	Employs growing conventionally-spelled word recognition vocabulary
Writing Sample:	tuth Fare wn nit I ws n mi BeD anD the tuth Fare cam.

Phase 4	(End of first grade or sooner)
Spelling/Sound Awareness Looks Like:	Spells many words correctly Operates with a chunking strategy when inventing unknown words (e.g., chunks phonics patterns) *buildings* spelled *BILLDINGS*; *everywhere* spelled *EVREWHAIR*
Word Reading Looks Like:	Reads over 100 words automatically Cues on chunks Accurately decodes nonsense words: *yode, fler, cleef* Recognizes syllable units in polysyllabic words: *man* in hu*man*; com*mand*
Guided Reading Looks Like:	Reads more independently without gradual release model Independent reading of Level G-I easy chapter books
Writing Looks Like:	Writes showing an awareness of phonics patterns Writes using conventional spelling patterns
Writing Sample:	My feet are filesh. I whair sis 3. My feet take me evrewhair. My feet like tu cline trees and billding I walk to school. My feet make me swem in water. My feet art tiyerd at the end of the day. **MY foot**

Notes

Notes